Physical Characteristics of the
Rat Terrier

(from the United Kennel Club's breed standard)

Body: Slightly longer than tall, and length of the front leg should approximately equal one-half of the dog's height. Whether the dog is standing or moving, the line of the back is strong and level. The loin is moderately short, slightly arched, and muscular, with moderate tuck-up. The croup is slightly sloping. Viewed from the side, the forechest extends in a shallow oval shape in front of the forelegs.

Tail: Set on at the end of the croup. The natural tail is thick at the base and tapers toward the tip.

Hindquarters: Muscular with the length of the upper and lower thighs being approximately equal. The angulation of the hindquarters is in balance with the angulation of the forequarters. The stifles are well-bent, and the hocks are well let down.

Height and Weight: *Miniature Variety:* Not exceeding 13 inches, measured at the withers. *Standard Variety:* Over 13 inches but not exceeding 18 inches, measured at the withers.

Coat: Short, dense, and smooth, with a sheen. Whiskers are not removed.

Feet: Compact and slightly oval in shape. The two middle toes are slightly longer than the other toes. Front dewclaws may be removed. Rear dewclaws must be removed.

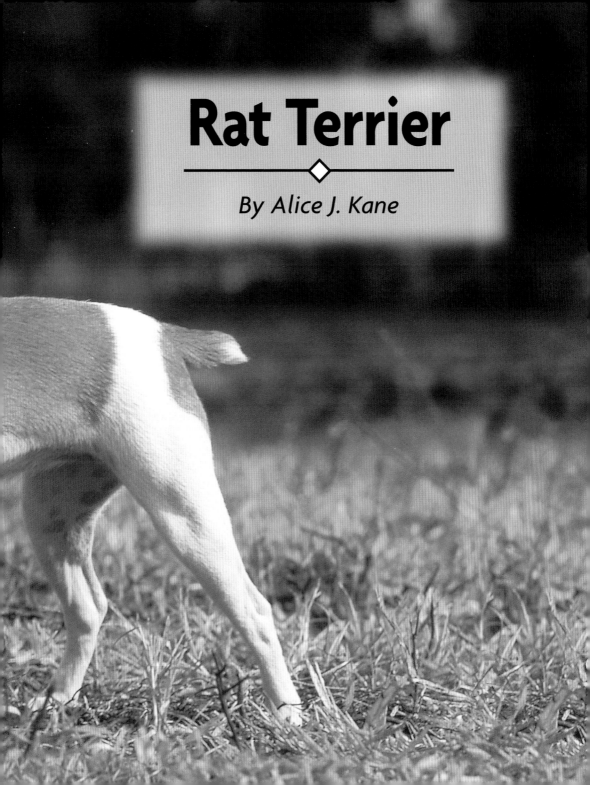

Rat Terrier

◇

By Alice J. Kane

9 History of the Rat Terrier

Unearth the origins of the truly feisty terrier, the Rat Terrier, at one time called the Feist. This British original gained its famed in the United States where it was used as a working farm dog and exterminator. Learn about famous Rat Terriers as well as related strains including the American Hairless Terrier, the Teddy Roosevelt Terrier and the Decker.

18 Characteristics of the Rat Terrier

Meet the dual-personality Rat Terrier, a hard-working, fearless terrier dog and a lovable lapful of impetuous charm. Once you surrender your home and heart to a Rat Terrier, you will be overwhelmed by the virtues and talents of this intelligent, industrious little dog. Find out if you are the right person to own this one-of-a-kind canine companion.

26 Breed Standard for the Rat Terrier

Learn the requirements of a well-bred Rat Terrier by studying the descriptions of the breed as set forth by the United Kennel Club. Both show dogs and pets must possess key characteristics as outlined in the standard.

34 Your Puppy Rat Terrier

Be advised about choosing a reputable breeder and selecting a healthy, typical puppy. Understand the responsibilities of ownership, including home preparation, acclimatization, the vet and prevention of common puppy problems.

56 Everyday Care of Your Rat Terrier

Enter into a sensible discussion of dietary and feeding considerations, exercise, grooming, traveling and identification of your dog. This chapter discusses Rat Terrier care for all stages of development.

74 Training Your Rat Terrier

By Charlotte Schwartz
Be informed about the importance of training your Rat Terrier from the basics of house-breaking and understanding the development of a young dog to executing obedience commands (sit, stay, down, etc.).

Contents

KENNEL CLUB BOOKS® RAT TERRIER
ISBN: 1-59378-367-1

Copyright © 2003, 2005 • Kennel Club Books, LLC
308 Main Street, Allenhurst, NJ 07711 USA
Cover Design Patented: US 6,435,559 B2 • Printed in South Korea

Photos by Isabelle Français with additional photographs by:
Norvia Behling, T. J. Calhoun, Carolina Biological Supply, Doskocil,
James Hayden-Yoav, James R. Hayden, RBP, Bill Jonas,
Dwight R. Kuhn, Dr. Dennis Kunkel, Mikki Pet Products, Phototake,
Jean Claude Revy, Alice Roche, Dr. Andrew Spielman and Alice van Kempen.

The owner wishes to thank the owners of the dogs featured in this book,
including Margaret Burz, Linda Hibbard, Cynthia Humphrey and Amanda Rogers.

Illustrations by Patricia Peters.

The Rat Terrier is a very active, healthy dog that requires any equally on-his-toes owner to keep pace with this dynamic companion dog.

HISTORY OF THE
RAT TERRIER

The feisty terrier! An expression heard so often in terrier talk, one might believe it was the name of an actual breed! But, down through the ages, only one terrier officially had the boldness and tenacity to claim the name as its own. The distinctive Feist originated in England in the 1820s. But even in England, his beginnings were more reflective of America's "melting pot," the country in which he later was developed as a distinct pure breed. Like the Americans who embraced him, his colorful ancestry was a "bit of this and that." Historians say that he was a cross of the Smooth Fox Terrier and the black and tan Manchester Terrier. But they go

DOCKING THE TAX
Over 200 years ago, English laws came into effect stating that dogs that worked for a living were exempt from tax. Working dogs were distinguished by the docking of the tail. The practice of tail docking on Rat Terriers has always been done to prevent risk of injury as they work.

EAR CROPPING

Ear cropping consists of surgically trimming the ear leathers and then training the ears to stand upright. The Rat Terrier's ears are never cropped. Originally, cropping was done to prevent the ears from being bitten by any adversary. With fighting dogs and terriers, cropped ears gave the opponent less to hang on to. Ear cropping also was considered important for cosmetic purposes, as it gives the dog a very smart look. In the US, dogs can be shown with cropped or natural ears, as is the case in most European nations. American breeders concentrate on the stylish look of cropped ears, which they believe give the dog's head a more appealing, sharper look. In fact, at most shows in the US, it is more difficult to do top winning with a dog with natural ears, though some pet owners favor the natural look.

back even further to those oldest breeds that comprise these two breeds and gave the Feist its uniqueness: the English White Terrier, now extinct, adding mild manner, gentility and nobility; the Black and Tan Terrier, adding hearty demeanor and keen senses; the Bull-and-Terrier, supplying feistiness, tenacity and stamina; and the Hinks' White Bull Terrier, creating true grit and gameness. The resultant new breed had coloring like the Manchester, black

body and face with tan trim on his cheeks and tan spots over the eyes. Demonstrating fearless tenacity, this hybrid became known as a Feist—a perfect title for this small, smart, hardy varmint dispatcher!

The breed won British fanciers almost immediately. This was a versatile dog, resourceful and determined, with a generous nature. Master of the hunt in the fields, the Feist also caught the eye of those in the less scrupulous sport of rat baiting. At that time, terriers were often pitted against other terriers, but the Feist's natural instinct to kill vermin created a new "sport." The dog was placed in a pit and hundreds of rats were poured down. Bets were wagered as to how many vermin the Feist could dispatch within a specified time. As ratting competitions became the favorite social events of royalty and commoners alike, many fell in love with this small terrier. But perhaps most captivated were the many American visitors who had never seen such a dog. The first Feists, or "ratting terriers," in the US appeared during the 1850s and '60s, but the vast majority of imports arrived in the 1890s. Old England's favorite ratter was about to become a truly American breed.

By the turn of the 19th

century, the United States was outgrowing its adolescence. Frontier living was giving way to civilized society and even country dwellers were no longer protecting their homes from bear! Hunters who had previously used bulldogs and curs for protection and guard now desired a dog that could trail and tree small game. The first Rat Terriers (Feists) were exclusively black and tan colored, ears buttoned over, medium-sized and approximately 18 pounds. Gaining popularity in the southern parts of the US, these imports easily adapted to different climates and terrain. They kept farms free of rats and fox and proved to be excellent hunters. From squirrels to cougar, they were quick, fierce and lethal.

But American Rat Terrier enthusiasts saw room for improvement and for the next 30 years, the Feist would be bred based primarily on function. Form would be a product of its purpose and development. The breed, in fact, underwent a process that would take it far from its original form in England.

Breeds were added to the Rat Terrier dependent on geography and required purpose of the dog. Those seeking a good hunting dog with more desire to be a companion brought about the re-introduction of the Smooth Fox Terrier, turning the breed into the black and white tricolored dog we see today. To further enhance his hunting prowess, he was crossed to the Beagle with its topnotch scenting ability. A stockier body and shortened legs were also favored for going to ground. With the addition of the Whippet and the Greyhound, breeders got a speedier hunter with better sighting ability and a slightly elongated body. They also added a wonderful range of new colors: red, liver, chocolate, brindle, black fawn and cream. But perhaps most important, these gentle breeds produced a mellower Feist, the temperament we see in today's Rat Terriers. Over time, the Chihuahua, Toy Fox Terrier and Toy Manchester were introduced to bring down the size considerably, accounting for the toy variety commonly seen today and also for new colors. These three toy breeds are, in

ABOUT 357 RATS PER HOUR

The Rat Terrier is astounding in his ratting abilities and the breed came to be known as the prince of the rat pits. Developed in Great Britain to be quick and fierce in the hunt, one ratting terrier named Billy was believed to have killed 2,501 rats in 7 hours in Suffolk!

THE TOY FOX COMPARISON

Given the many shapes and sizes of the Rat Terrier over its history in the US, the breed has often been confused with other breeds like the Jack Russell Terrier (which is not as refined as the Rat Terrier) and the Toy Fox Terrier. This latter breed is indeed similar in some respects, but different in many others. The Toy Fox Terrier never weighs over 7 pounds, while the giant Rat Terrier can weigh as much as 35 pounds; albeit the toy variety can weigh a mere 4 to 6 pounds. The outline of the Toy Fox is squarer than the longer body of the Rat Terrier, and the topline slopes slightly, which is not a characteristic of the straight back of the Toy Fox. There are also differences in the eyes and ears of the two breeds. The Rat Terrier has V-shaped ears that can be erect, tipped or button, while the Toy Fox are always erect and set more to the sides. The eyes are more obliquely set in the Rat Terrier, compared to the forward placed eyes of the Toy Fox.

fact, considered among the most influential of the breeds added to the makeup of the Rat Terrier. The new improved breed was indeed a winner! The Rat Terrier was a hunter with a 100-yard range—hunters could follow on foot while he trailed and treed small game; he was a watchdog with keen sight and smell; and, finally, he was what his breeders and fans fervently pursued—a devoted and generous companion dog.

Changes in place, this newly Americanized little terrier was positioned for prestige. He found it in the home of America's "royal family." In 1901, President Theodore Roosevelt moved into a White House infested with mice and rats. The mansion was filled with traps and poisons, but the vermin seemed immune. Little did Teddy Roosevelt realize he was naming a breed when he set his favorite trusty little Feist terriers on the case! Ridding the White House of pesky vermin,

---

AMERICAN HAIRLESS TERRIER

For over three decades, a variety of hairless Rat Terriers has been in the making. The beginnings of this variety traces to Willie and Edwin Scott of Louisiana, who encountered a hairless mutant in a litter of Rat Terriers. This pup, called Josephine, was bred to produce more hairless progeny, a feat that was finally accomplished after several litters. Trout Creek Kennel was established in 1981, after nine years of concerted effort by the Scotts.

Unlike other hairless dogs such as the Chinese Crested and Mexican Hairless who have tufts of hair on their heads, feet and tail, the hairless Rat Terrier is completely bald, except for his whisker and eyebrows. All hairless breeds suffer from skin problems (due to the lack of coat and the exposure to the sun). Poor dentition is another characteristic of most hairless breeds, though the hairless Rat Terrier possesses a very strong compliment of teeth.

The American Hairless Terrier, the name reserved for these dogs, possesses a recessive gene for hairlessness, which differs from the genetic base for other such breeds that have a lethal dominant gene. The coated Rat Terrier, however, is still used in hairless breeding programs from time to time. Until a sufficient gene pool is established, the hairless Rat Terrier continues to be a "work in progress." The UKC will recognize the American Hairless Terrier when this goal is finally reached.

Depending on the association with which your Rat Terrier is registered, a hairless Rat Terrier may or may not be shown. The Rat Terrier Club of America does not permit such dogs to compete, while the UKC-affiliated American Rat Terrier Association does allow the hairless variety to participate. For more information on the hairless variety, contact the American Hairless Rat Terrier Club.

this sporting little breed earned the name it has today—"Rat Terrier." The dog named Skip, Roosevelt's favorite, was the perfect companion to keep up with this high-energy President. On the hunt or in the home, this loyal ratter never left his side.

The breed's popularity soared throughout the 1930s and '40s. They were so common on American farms that it seemed there was one on every porch! But by the 1950s, the family farm was undergoing major changes. Pesticides and new poisons, along with mechanized farming, displaced the need for a "common farm dog." Along

with a growing public interest in pure-bred dogs, the Rat Terrier was in jeopardy of suffering extinction—the fate of his oldest ancestor, the Old English White Terrier, the dog that all of the present English terrier breeds have descended from.

But the tenacious Rat Terrier held on to its following. Years of skilled and devoted breeding had produced a utility dog that both sports people and dog-loving families were determined to keep by their side. This small number of loyal breeders continued to breed for working skills, type and temperament. Utilizing outcrosses when necessary, this "breed of many breeds" was more than saved, and his attributes were refined and perfected. Historically, an excellent, energetic friend of the hunter, by the 1990s, his intelligence, loyalty and genetic soundness have made him a perfect companion for the pet owner. The Rat Terrier has made an amazing

The Jack Russell Terrier is often confused with the Rat Terrier. Jack Russells appear in smooth and wire coats.

comeback. In the US, there are not only highly active breed clubs but also a recognized standard. Having made the leap from "strain" to recognized breed on January 1, 1999, the Rat Terrier was officially recognized by the United Kennel Club (UKC).

As a "breed of many breeds," it is perhaps not surprising that today's Rat Terriers are often individual in both looks and characteristics. Due to limited breeding stock, many Rat Terriers were bred to other breeds of dogs such as Toy Fox Terriers, Chihuahuas and Jack Russell Terriers. The infusion of these breeds produced a Rat Terrier with short legs and a longer body; this variety is called the Teddy Roosevelt Terrier. While it retains the same desirable characteristics as the longer legged Rat Terrier, inter-breeding of the two varieties is discouraged and the Teddy Roosevelt Terrier has a separate standard, which also was approved by the UKC in 1999.

The UKC also recognizes a variety of hairless Rat Terriers. These dogs are free from hair except for whiskers and guard hairs on the muzzle and eyebrows. In 1972, the first hairless Rat Terrier was born to Willie and Edwina Scott of Louisiana. A coatless puppy in a

FARMHAND FOR HIRE
Throughout the 1930s and '40s, practically no farm was without one of these trusty little dogs then called the "squirrel dog" and "old-time fox terrier." To many a farmer, this alert, loyal and tenacious utility dog was simply top farmhand!

litter of normal-coated siblings, "Josephine" was prized by the Scotts, and after a nine-year effort, this little female whelped a final litter that included two hairless and two coated puppies. This "blessed event" became the basis of Trout Creek Kennel and a full-scale breeding program of hairless terriers. Today, the hairless Rat Terrier bloodlines still require carefully planned mating to coated Rat Terriers.

In the United States, the breed is currently shown in the UKC as a variety of the Rat Terrier, but hairless terrier fanciers anticipate the time when the breed's gene pool will be sufficient to present these "hairless cousins" as its own breed. Already given an official name—the American Hairless Terrier—the breed now has its own club in America. The American Hairless Rat Terrier Club has a very active membership and keeps fanciers busy with its own special events, while awaiting UKC approval of separate breed status.

The other variety of smooth-coated, compact "Feisty" terriers traditionally comes in three different sizes, Standard, Mid-Sized and Toy. But for UKC conformation shows, the Rat Terrier is divided into two varieties: Miniature, not exceeding 13 inches, and Standard, not exceeding 18 inches.

It is noteworthy to mention yet another strain of Rat Terrier, the larger Decker, developed by a sportsman enthusiast from Oregon. In 1970, Milton Decker, an avid hunter, began his own hunt for a Rat Terrier extraordinaire—a strain that would

> **UNDERCOVER HUNTERS**
> During the Middle Ages, commoners were prohibited from hunting in the royal forests. If found, they would be severely punished. However, their crafty Rat Terriers—easily hidden and savvy in evading capture—were perfect hunting dogs. Many a poor farmer was kept from starving by his loyal terrier companion.

become his "ideal" of an already ideal dog. Decker saw this perfection in his large Rat Terrier, Henry, a 32-pound dog as eager to please his family in the home or on the hunt. Traveling across the United States, Decker sought the largest Rat Terriers he could find for breeding stock. With precision and patience, a strain was created that retained the large size, plus "super-sized" the other traits that makes the Rat Terrier so prized—from natural hunting instincts to extreme intelligence to quiet demeanor.

To be considered a Decker, the dog must carry the original Decker bloodlines throughout its pedigree. The standards are the same as the Rat Terrier but the strain possesses its own particular "look" in skull (slightly rounded and broad on top between ears), muzzle (wedge shaped and squaring at the nose) and ears (erect, usually by ten weeks of age). With colors of

Whether Standard or Miniature, Rat Terriers think they are king-sized dogs with no task or foe too large!

A TOUCH OF THE "IG"

The Italian Greyhound cross gave the Rat Terrier an elongated body, a calmer temperament and the skills of the sighthound. If not for the cross, Rat Terriers would be almost identical to the Jack Russell Terrier. Breeders work to maintain the sweet easygoing nature of the Rat Terrier.

black/white/tan, tan and white, or black and tan, the Decker strain can range from 16 to 19 inches in height and from 22-40 pounds in weight. Decker enthusiasts say that the strain has the same character and devotion to its family as the Rat Terrier, but it can be a bit more aloof and independent.

RAT TERRIER

A FEROCIOUS LAP DOG?

Don't be fooled by the Rat Terrier's aggressive, seemingly ferocious behavior on the hunt. A Rat Terrier's main purpose in life is to be with his family, preferably on a warm lap! He would, in fact, be an ideal volunteer visitor to a nursing home, where lap-curling and doting on new friends would greatly please him!

Meet the "Feist," more commonly known today as the Rat Terrier. Hunter. Farm worker. Keen watch-dog. Pound for pound, this compact, busy little dog finds no job too big or too small. He was dubbed the "Feist" for his fearless determination on the hunt but, with a heart many times his size, today's Rat Terrier would just as soon stalk your affection. He loves his home and his family above all and will put all his work aside for the bliss of human companion-ship. Return that affection and you will have a friend for life.

Breeders will tell you that while most dogs think they are human, Rat Terriers know that they are! On the hunt, on the farm—or nestled in your arms—the Rat Terrier is at your service. Generations of breeding for a sporting companion has produced what breeders call the perfect "dual-personality" dog. His grit and gameness "on-the-job" gives way instantly in the home. Suddenly, this unlikely lap dog enjoys nothing more than a comforting cuddle. Sure of himself, but eager to please, lively but not hyper, protective but not aggressive, the Rat Terrier ranks high as a household companion. Above all else, this breed wants the pleasure of your company. Giving you that foxy smile, tail thumping in excitement, he lets you know that you are number one in his world. This is a dog with charm. And he knows it!

The sporting Rat Terrier is also thrilled to have a job—the better to show his undying devotion to his owner. Dubbed the "squirrel dog," the Rat Terrier possesses strong prey instincts that will keep your farm free of vermin, squirrels, raccoons and rabbits; he can even flush out game birds. Hunting enthusiasts say they are unequalled as "jump dogs" for deer in brushy regions. Jumping and chasing them, the Rat Terrier barks triumphantly as he runs to his master. But talk to those hunters and they will tell you that this terrier is favored most for his sweet easygoing manner and his will to please and be near. The Rat Terrier craves civilization and socialization. Sports person or pet owner, return his unwavering devotion and you will get back unconditional love.

While the breed was developed as a working terrier, those who loved the Rat Terrier put much thought into molding his disposition. Tenacity, stamina and keen senses were balanced by good temperament and mild manner. That combination

BRIGHT AND WILLING
The Rat Terrier is highly intelligent and resourceful, and his love to please helps him excel in obedience and agility trials. Working together with your dog will build the human/canine bond and keep your smart little terrier from getting bored.

remains critical to breeders, today. "Master of the hunt," but always home companion. Feisty in the field, but still a lovable lapful.

To add to his canine perfection, breeders have produced an easy-maintenance dog. The short-haired Rat Terrier, apart from natural shedding, is blessed with a naturally clean appearance,

Too friendly and too much fun, the Rat Terrier is an outgoing "feisty" terrier who can get along with other dogs if properly introduced.

requiring only an occasional bath. A brisk brushing helps the shedding process in the spring and fall.

The virtues of the Rat Terrier are endless. While early admirers praised his work capability, his love of human companions and sensitivity make him an ideal family dog.

The Rat Terrier does very well with young and old, although, as with any other dog, children should be quietly introduced and taught to show their companion kindness and respect. Those dogs raised with children are particularly patient and tolerant and make wonderful family companions. The Rat Terrier is generous in his love for all family members,

although it is not uncommon for a dog to choose a special person and bond particularly close to that lucky favorite.

Some Rat Terrier owners claim that their dogs talk to them, alerting them to the approach of dinner hour, or, perhaps, to an unreasonable period of being ignored! While they do not usually bark unnecessarily, they are extremely intelligent and social and have no hesitation

A TALKATIVE TERRIER

Rat Terriers are not mindless yappers, but they can be demanding, using their paws and mumbling and grumbling when they are ignored. They will talk to you to help you see their point!

reminding you that that their job is that of companion dog!

Proud of his terrier heritage, your Rat Terrier may also yip his concern to you at would-be intruders at the door. He is extremely alert and sensitive to strange sounds and makes a good watchdog, defending family property. Even well-adjusted Rat Terriers may be reserved with strangers at first. But most will play polite host in the home and quickly respond to kind strangers, as long as you are there to reassure him.

The Rat Terrier may be feisty on the hunt, but unlike many terriers, he is a lover, not a fighter. Not only is he not dog-aggressive, but some owners claim he often finds himself in trouble for being too friendly. Full of fun, your Rat Terrier may see every potential dog as a playmate. You should therefore exercise caution in such social situations. Once provoked to fight, your Rat Terrier will not back down! They are small but sturdy dogs and you must never forget that they are terriers.

Most do well in a multiple-dog family, and apart from spats over food or hoarding toys or who gets the bed, they will co-exist peacefully with other family dogs. They possess pack instincts, and company will help prevent problems with separation anxiety. Breeders recommend that you do not get more than one Rat Terrier

at a time. Two puppies may tend to bond with each other rather than with you. Once your first dog is properly bonded and socialized is a better time to bring a second puppy into your household. This will also reduce pack order dominance problems between your Rat Terriers.

As for other family or neighborhood pets, keep in mind that being a terrier, his glee in the chase will not enamor him to cats, birds, rabbits or other small mammals. That said, if you raise

A MOMENT'S POUT

Naturally well mannered and easily controlled by the owner's voice, the Rat Terrier rarely requires other discipline. Wrongly scolded or feeling bereft of attention, your dog may pout, but he loves you too much to pout for long!

your dog with these other pets, he will most likely accept them as a part of his family.

Watching a Rat Terrier at play is topnotch entertainment! His frenzied escapades around the yard are as much fun for you as they are for him. But a Rat Terrier's high spirits should always be contained within a fenced area. He is a natural escape artist and his courage sometimes overrides his sense of safety. Owners should keep a sharp eye on amusing shenanigans that can lead to trouble.

Any Rat Terrier breeder will first tell you that this is a highly sensitive dog. A Rat Terrier wants nothing more than to learn your language, tune in to your needs and anticipate what makes you happy. Look into the eyes of your terrier and you will see the gratitude, wonder and joy he takes in being your special friend. His faith in you will never waver and you will want to deserve that trust by providing him with a life of emotional happiness and well-being. Key to this is keeping him in the home, actively involved with family life. A Rat Terrier should never be kept outside in a kennel. He may love the outdoors, but human contact is his reason for being. Only if allowed by your side will he thrive mentally and physically. Your Rat Terrier has a keen, alert brain and can learn almost anything you take the time

to teach him. He may also use that brain to demonstrate a sense of humor, to have a bit of irreverent fun with you to see if you can take a joke!

Because this is a highly intelligent breed, training and supervised play are crucial to getting the best out of your relationship. From the day you welcome him home, touch your Rat Terrier frequently, gently playing with his feet and face, getting him used to being handled by family members. Enjoy some rough-and-tumble playtime with him. He is a terrier! Play and handling are not only perfect opportunities to bond with your new dog but also are stimulating activity for his energetic mind and body. A busy terrier is a happy, easier-to-live-with terrier!

Like any smart dog, the Rat Terrier will quickly size up who is boss. Setting boundaries right at the beginning will give him reasonable guidelines to follow and make him eager to please you. It is much like raising a child—a relationship of mutual respect is

---

SHAKE AND TOSS
Rat Terriers efficiently rid a farm of mice with a vigorous shake and a toss over the shoulder. If the amount gets overwhelming, what can't be put immediately into the mouth, gets pinned down with paws until the vermin can be properly dispensed with!

Rat Terriers do not perceive themselves to be any smaller than even the biggest Rottweiler. This fearless fellow, up on his hinds, is sniffing out the plaster competition.

key to building a strong bond. "No" means no. "Sit" means sit. Now! Say it only once. If you say it 100 times, your dog will learn to wait until you say it 99 times! So give the command and if your Rat Terrier doesn't understand—or

EARNING THEIR KEEP

The Rat Terrier is the picture of good health. Many vets claim that they would starve to death if they were dependent on Rat Terrier business! Hardy and robust, Rat Terriers leap, dash, chase and are happiest when they get to earn their keep. Give them any job at all and you will bring out their best.

is being obstinate—gently but firmly enforce it. Above all, do praise him highly and exuberantly for making the right decisions (aka "obeying"). A treat, toys, hugs—whatever he loves best—is his reward for being a good dog. Positive reinforcement, not punishment, is the very best method of training a plucky, loving Rat Terrier. Training is not a battle of wits, a challenge to see "who's in charge." It is the establishment of a lifetime relationship, and it may also save your dog's life. Responding quickly to a command such as "Drop it" or "Down" has saved many dogs from poisoning or physical injuries on the street.

Perhaps the greatest bonus of having a trained Rat Terrier in your home is the delight of a canine companion who has learned the fun and rewards of pleasing you. Terriers rarely make the list of the most obedient dogs, but don't let this little character fool you. He is perfectly trainable. If he loves you, he will love to please you and will delight in a working partnership as much as you do. This is a hardy terrier with attitude and unflagging energy. He is a "can do" dog and would like nothing more than for you to do it with him!

The Rat Terrier enjoys an average lifespan of 12 to 18 years. While basically healthy and not prone to illness, some terriers may

suffer allergies (contact, inhalants and foods). Some individuals may be sensitive to certain anesthesia, something to be considered in electing surgical procedures not absolutely necessary. Another problem that may occur is demodectic mange, treated with topical salves, dips and drug therapies. Overall, however, this is a hardy and long-lived breed.

As with any other breed, if you know your Rat Terrier well, you will be alert to any signals of ill health. Appetite, thirst, activity level, toilet habits, etc., are all signs of your dog's well-being. As he gets older, watch for teeth, eye and ear problems and also swellings under the skin. One of the benefits of regular grooming sessions with your Rat Terrier is getting to know his body so that you can quickly detect any changes that may need checking. Luckily, this breed, like most other terriers, has a marvelous constitution, and you can expect your companion to lead you on a merry chase for many years.

RAT TERRIER

The Rat Terrier can be registered by numerous registries, but, at this time, is only recognized by one major kennel club, the United Kennel Club (UKC). The Rat Terrier is not yet an American Kennel Club officially recognized breed and may only be shown where "Rare Breeds" are specifically invited. Rat Terriers are registered by numerous registries, the majority of which are pedigree services, which record the lineage/pedigree of an individual dog, but do not offer nationally sanctioned competitions, events or titles.

Each breed recognized by the UKC has an approved standard that tells us what the dog should look like and what we should expect from his temperament. A good breeder works to produce dogs that meet this standard, to assure that the breed you admire today will continue to thrive and improve in future generations. While the perfect dog has yet to be born, those devoted to the Rat Terrier work tirelessly to produce it! They cherish the characteristics that make their breed different from other terriers and are proud

to tell you exactly what those are. The approved standard, meticulously put together by breed fanciers and specialists, gives you a brief but all-important picture of the dog you are taking home with you.

While the standard's characteristics describe a fearless, tenacious hunter with seemingly unlimited energy, the charm of the Rat Terrier is in his exceptionally friendly nature. He enjoys human companionship immensely and will enthusiastically share any activity with his owner. These are personality traits actually written into the standard, proof that those involved with the breed are as concerned with temperament as they are with appearance.

Dog shows are a wonderful opportunity to observe ideal examples of the Rat Terrier. In no way beauty pageants, dog shows determine how closely each dog in the ring conforms to his ideal as described in the breed standard. Here, you will see the Rat Terrier as close to perfection as today's breeder can produce, not only in soundness and appearance but also in attitude. As the Rat Terrier struts around the ring, he fairly vibrates with a sense of self importance, daring the judge not to "Pick me!"

The Rat Terrier breed standard reflects the breeders' ideals and desire to perpetuate this fine, spirited little terrier through the generations. Equipped with an understanding of this standard and an overall picture of the breed, the new owner can know what to expect from his Rat Terrier and how to best meet his needs.

Following is an excerpt from the official standard for the Rat Terrier as accepted by the United Kennel Club.

UNITED KENNEL CLUB STANDARD FOR THE RAT TERRIER

General Appearance: The Rat Terrier is a muscular, active, small-to-medium hunting terrier. The preferred ratio of length of body (prosternum to point of buttocks) to height (withers to ground) to is 10:9. The head is broad, slightly domed, wedge-shaped, and proportionate to the size of the body. Ears are V-shaped, set at the outside edges of the skull, and may be erect or button. Both varieties may have a natural tail carried in an upward curve. The Coated variety may have a docked or natural bob tail. The Rat Terrier comes in solid white, other solid colors with markings, and white with a variety of colored patches. *Disqualification:* A short-legged dog whose proportions vary significantly from the 10:9 ratio lacks breed type and must be disqualified.

Characteristics: The Rat Terrier is an energetic, alert dog whose curiosity and intelligence make him easy to train. The Rat Terrier has sometimes been described as having a dual personality. He is a fearless, tenacious hunter with seemingly unlimited energy. When he is not hunting, however, the Rat Terrier is an exceptionally friendly companion, getting along well with children, other dogs,

The Rat Terrier's head should form a blunt wedge, when viewed from the front, as exhibited by this handsome specimen.

A Standard,
Coated Rat
Terrier with a
docked tail and
prick ears. He is
correctly
balanced, of
correct structure
and type.

A Standard, Coated Rat Terrier with a docked tail and prick ears. He is correctly balanced, of correct structure and type.

and even cats. Rat Terriers enjoy human companionship immensely and will enthusiastically share any activity with their owners. Rat Terriers should not be sparred during conformation judging.

Head: The head is proportionate to the size of the body. When viewed from the side, the skull and muzzle are of equal length and joined by a moderate stop. Viewed from the front and the side, the Rat Terrier's head forms a blunt wedge shape. *Fault:* Abrupt stop. *Skull*—The skull is broad and slightly domed. It tapers slightly toward the muzzle. The jaws are powerful with well-muscled cheeks. *Serious fault:* Apple head. *Muzzle*—The muzzle is well filled-out under the eyes, well-chiseled, and tapers slightly from the stop to the nose. Jaws are powerful and hinged well back, allowing the dog to open his mouth wide enough to catch rats and other rodents. Lips are dry and tight with no flews. Lip pigment matches nose pigment. *Fault:* Snipey muzzle. *Teeth*—The Rat Terrier has a

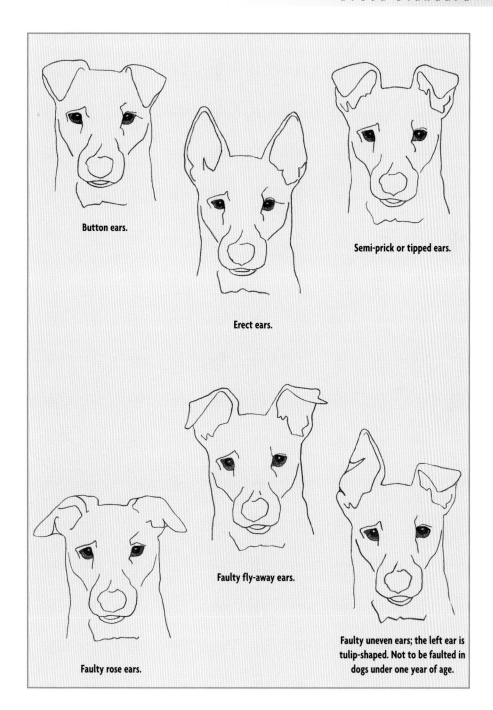

Button ears.

Erect ears.

Semi-prick or tipped ears.

Faulty fly-away ears.

Faulty rose ears.

Faulty uneven ears; the left ear is tulip-shaped. Not to be faulted in dogs under one year of age.

complete set of good-sized, evenly spaced, white teeth. A scissors bite is preferred but a level bite is acceptable. *Faults:* Missing teeth; overshot or undershot bite. *Nose—* The nose is black or self-colored. *Faults:* Dudley or butterfly nose. *Eyes—*Eyes are set obliquely and are round, small, and somewhat prominent. Eyerims match nose pigment. *Coated Variety:* Eye color ranges from dark brown to amber and corresponds with coat color. Hazel eyes are acceptable in dogs with lighter coat color. Blue or amber eyes are permitted in blue-colored dogs only, but a dark gray eye with gray eyerims is preferred. *Hairless Variety:* Eyes may be any acceptable color. *Faults:* Bulgy eyes; deep-set eyes; light-colored eyes in a dog with black coat color or black pigment; both eyes not of matching colors; eye with iris containing more than one color; wall or china eye. *Ears—*Ears are V-shaped, set at the outside edges of the skull. Matching ears are strongly preferred. Non-matching ear carriage should be penalized to the degree of the variation. *Note:* Ear carriage may not stabilize until a dog is mature. Dogs under one year of age should not be penalized for variations in ear carriage. *Coated Variety:* Ears are either erect, tipped, or button when the dog is alert. *Hairless Variety:* Erect ears are preferred but tipped or button ears are acceptable. *Faults:* Erect ears with the sides curved inward forming a shape like a tulip petal; rose ears; flying ears; non-matching ear carriages. *Disqualification:* Hanging ears.

Neck: The neck is clean, moderately long, muscular, slightly arched, and tapers slightly from the shoulders to the head. The neck blends smoothly into well laid back shoulders.

Forequarters: Shoulders are smoothly muscled. The shoulder blades are well laid back with the upper tips fairly close together at the withers. The upper arm appears to be equal in length to the shoulder blade and joins it at an apparent right angle. The elbows are close to the body. Viewed from any angle, the forelegs are straight, strong, and sturdy in bone. The pasterns are strong, short, and nearly vertical.

Body: A properly proportioned Rat Terrier is slightly longer (measured from prosternum to point of buttocks) than tall (measured from the withers to the ground), and length of the front leg (measured from point of elbow to the ground) should approximately equal one-half of the dog's height. Whether the dog is standing or moving, the line of the back is strong and level. The loin is moderately short, slightly arched, and muscular, with moderate tuck-up. The croup is slightly sloping. The ribs extend well back and are well sprung out from the spine, forming a broad, strong back, then curving down and inward to form a deep body. The brisket extends to or just below the elbow. Viewed from the front, the chest between the forelegs is well filled and of moderate width. Viewed from the side, the fore-chest extends in a shallow oval shape in front of the forelegs.

Hindquarters: The hindquarters are muscular with the length of the upper and lower thighs being approximately equal. The angulation of the hindquarters is in balance with the angulation of the forequarters. The stifles are well-bent, and the hocks are well let down. When the dog is standing, the short, strong rear pasterns are perpendicular to the ground and, viewed from the rear, parallel to one another.

Feet: The feet are compact and slightly oval in shape. The two middle toes are slightly longer than the other toes. Toes may be well split up but not flat or splayed. Front dewclaws may be removed. Rear dewclaws must be removed. *Faults:* Flat feet; splayed feet; rear dewclaws present.

Tail: The tail is set on at the end of the croup. The natural tail is thick at the base and tapers toward the tip. When the dog is alert, the tail is carried in an upward curve. When relaxed, the tail may be carried straight out behind the dog. *Coated Variety:* A docked or natural bob tail is preferred, but a natural tail is not a fault. Docking should be

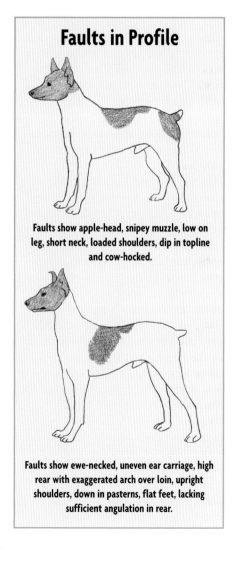

Faults in Profile

Faults show apple-head, snipey muzzle, low on leg, short neck, loaded shoulders, dip in topline and cow-hocked.

Faults show ewe-necked, uneven ear carriage, high rear with exaggerated arch over loin, upright shoulders, down in pasterns, flat feet, lacking sufficient angulation in rear.

A comparison of the Standard and the Miniature. The Standard on the left should be 13-18 inches, button ears, preferred docked tail and smooth coated. The Miniature on the right should be under 13 inches, Hairless variety, with preferred prick ears and undocked tail. These are the preferences for the hairless variety.

between the second and third joint of the tail. *Hairless Variety:* A natural tail is strongly preferred. A docked or natural bob tail in this variety is a serious fault. *Faults (Both Varieties):* Bent tail; ring tail.

Coat: *Coated Variety:* The coat is short, dense, and smooth, with a sheen. Whiskers are not removed. *Hairless Variety:* Puppies are born with a soft, vestigial down that generally covers the body. This "down" gradually diminishes until age six to eight weeks, by which time the pup should be completely hairless. A mature Rat Terrier, Hairless variety, is free from hair except for whiskers and guard hairs on the muzzle, and eyebrows. Short, very fine (vellus) hair may be present on the body of a mature dog. The skin is smooth and warm to the touch. The Hairless variety may

sweat when overheated or stressed, but this is not to be faulted in the ring. *Serious faults:* Vellus hair longer than 1 mm on a dog over six months of age. *Disqualifications (Both Varieties):* Wire or broken coat; long coat.

Color: *Coated Variety:* The coated Rat Terrier may be solid white, bi-color or tri-color but must always have some white, which may be of any size and located anywhere on the dog. The white area may be ticked as long as white predominates. The remaining accepted colors are: black, tan (ranging from dark tan to very light tan and from intense dark mahogany red to light red with black nose and eyerims), chocolate (ranging from dark liver to light chocolate with self-colored nose and eyerims), blue and blue fawn (with self-colored nose and eyerims), apricot (ranging from orange to faded yellow with black nose and eyerims), and lemon (ranging from orange to faded yellow with self-colored nose and eyerims). Colored areas may have sable overlay. *Faults:* Fawn (pale yellowish tan with self-colored nose), cream (pale yellow to off-white), fallow with black mask (very light yellowish tan with black mask), and silver (the extreme dilution of blue). *Disqualifications*: Brindle; merle; absence of white; any solid color other than white. *Hairless Variety:* Any skin color is acceptable. The skin is usually parti-colored with an underlying skin color and freckles or spots of contrasting color. Freckles enlarge with age, and skin color will darken when exposed to the sun. *Disqualification (Both Varieties):* Albinism.

Height and Weight: The Rat Terrier is divided into two varieties for conformation exhibition: Miniature and Standard. *Miniature Variety:* Not exceeding 13 inches, measured at the withers. *Standard Variety:* Over 13 inches but not exceeding 18 inches, measured at the withers.

Weight will vary depending on the size of the individual dog. Rat Terriers are working terriers and should be presented in hard, muscular condition.

Faults: Height over 19 inches; obesity.

Gait: The Rat Terrier moves with a jaunty air that suggests agility, speed, and power. Rat Terrier gait is smooth and effortless, with good reach of forequarters without any trace of hackney gait. Rear quarters have strong driving power, with hocks fully extending. Viewed from any position, legs turn neither in nor out, nor do feet cross or interfere with each other. As speed increases, feet tend to converge toward center line of balance.

Disqualifications: Unilateral or bilateral cryptorchid. Viciousness or extreme shyness. Unilateral or bilateral deafness. A short-legged dog whose proportions vary significantly from the 10:9 ratio. Hanging ears. Wire or broken coat. Long coat. Albinism. In the Coated variety: Brindle. Merle. Bi-color where neither color is white. Any solid color other than white.

Accomplished and attractive, this is "Millie," officially known as International Champion and UKC Grand Champion Lakeview's Running' The Mill, owned by Mindy McElhone.

RAT TERRIER

Assuming you have done research, gone to a couple of dog shows and studied the Rat Terrier standard, you are ready to embark on the beginning of a 12- to 18-year relationship with a loving living being. You should also expect to embark on a relationship with the breeder. Choosing a Rat Terrier means committing yourself to the care and training of a sporting, sensitive, people-loving breed. A good breeder will and should scrutinize you to see if you are up to the job. Just as you deserve a breeder with ethics and the best possible reputation, the breeder needs to know that his puppy will have the family life he has been bred for. A loving relationship between owner and dog is all-important, but also of concern is how the dog will fit into your lifestyle. You may have to convince the breeder that you have the time and willingness to meet the needs of a dog that requires the love of his human family even more than he needs his own kind. Once the breeder approves of you owning one of his Rat Terrier pups, you will be grateful for the relationship. This

PEDIGREE VS. REGISTRATION CERTIFICATE
Too often new owners are confused between these two important documents. Your puppy's pedigree, essentially a family tree, is a written record of a dog's genealogy of three generations or more. The pedigree will show you the names as well as performance titles of all dogs in your pup's background. Your breeder must provide you with a registration application, with his part properly filled out. You must complete the application and send it to the UKC with the proper fee. Every puppy must come from a litter that has been UKC-registered by the breeder, born in the USA and from a sire and dam that are also registered with the UKC.

The seller must provide you with complete records to identify the puppy. It's also helpful for the seller to provide the buyer with the following: breed; sex, color and markings; date of birth; litter number (when available); names and registration numbers of the parents; breeder's name; and date sold or delivered.

is the person you will turn to over and over again with anxious questions, small calamities and joyous milestones.

The UKC, National Rat Terrier Association and other breed clubs can give you names of reputable breeders in your area. Dog shows are ideal places to observe the breed and talk to breeders who take great pride in their Rat Terriers and enjoy the chance to share their enthusiasm with interested newcomers. Do visit with breeders after they are finished competing. Showing a dog takes much preparation and concentration and they will have more time to spend with you and answer your questions after the competition is over. Be prepared to wait for the breeder and dog you want. Good breeders often have waiting lists—but there is a reason for that. They have good dogs! The wait will be worth it.

Choosing from a litter is an exciting, often emotional, time. While the breeder should help you select the puppy best for you, it is wise to know some of the physical traits to look for. If physical traits are important to you, make sure the young puppy is free of faults. Basically, look for a head slightly rounded and moderately narrow. The muzzle should be well filled-out under the eyes and taper to the nose while being shorter than that of a Fox Terrier. Ears should be V-shaped, and

YOUR SCHEDULE . . .

If you lead an erratic, unpredictable life, with daily or weekly changes in your work requirements, consider the problems of owning a puppy. The new puppy has to be fed regularly, socialized (loved, petted, handled, introduced to other people) and, most importantly, allowed to go outdoors for house-training. As the dog gets older, he can be more tolerant of deviations in his feeding and relief schedule.

BOY OR GIRL?

An important consideration to be discussed is the sex of your puppy. For a family companion, a bitch may be the better choice, considering the female's inbred concern for all young creatures and her accompanying tolerance and patience. It is always advisable to spay a pet bitch, which may guarantee her a longer life.

either erect or button when the dog is alert, but do not expect ear carriage to stabilize until the dog is mature. Breeders explain that they just "pop up" one day! Ears should never be cropped. Eyes should be dark, warm and as near to circular or almond-shaped as possible. Tail should be natural bob (born with shortened tail) or docked between the second and third joint. Natural long tails are not normally preferred nor favored excepting in the Hairless variety.

The shorthaired Rat Terrier can show off quite vivid spotted patterns. Many are white with black-spotted markings with tan or rust trimming. But white, black, tan red and/or sable in any combination is acceptable. And mask markings on the head and face are highly prized.

Those with allergies might consider choosing the Hairless variety. A high percentage of allergy-sensitive persons do amazingly well tolerating these soft, smooth-skinned little terriers. Puppies are born with a soft down, but that diminishes between six and eight weeks. The mature Hairless will be free from hair, except for whiskers and guard hairs on the muzzle and eyebrows. Any color is acceptable and the adult's skin is often parti-colored with freckles and spots of contrasting color. The Hairless Rat Terrier has been a wonderful solution for dog-loving families with allergic members!

Temperament is, of course, what you and the breeder will be looking for in a companion dog, and it makes good sense to tap the breeder's experience and intuition. The breeder has seen the litter interact and knows the bold puppy, scrambling for first dibs at human attention. Or the timid puppy, sweet, but needing a little coercion to join in the fun. The Rat Terrier, male or female, is an inquisitive, outgoing breed, but each has his or her unique personality and approach to life. No one personality is right for all owners. The breeder can help you select the pup that will blend best into your own personal lifestyle.

Both males and females make wonderful pets. In the Rat Terrier breed, a neutered male will make as excellent a housedog as a female. In fact, both males and females can be territorial and tend to mark, so neutering and spaying is highly advised for both sexes.

If the breeder has the puppies' parents on the premises, you should see them as well as the litter. Observing the sire and dam will give you some idea of what you can expect when your puppy grows into an adult dog. Just as in people, physical and emotional traits are passed on from generation to generation. Some Rat Terrier breeders take pride in producing working dogs, capable

"BETTER SHOP AROUND!"

Finding a reputable breeder who sells healthy pups is very important, but make sure that the breeder you choose is not only someone you respect but also someone with whom you feel comfortable. Your breeder will be a resource long after you buy your puppy, and you must be able to call with reasonable questions without being made to feel like a pest! If you don't connect on a personal level, investigate some other breeders before making a final decision.

of stamina in the field. Others happily see their litters off to good homes in the city. The devoted Rat Terrier breeders you visit have worked diligently to produce well-bred, well-socialized puppies. Now, their hope is to provide them with the best possible lives. When you have been "chosen" to take a puppy home, you should have all the breeder's blessings and support.

ARE YOU PREPARED?

Unfortunately, when a puppy is bought by someone who does not take into consideration the time and attention that dog ownership requires, it is the puppy who suffers when he is either abandoned or placed in a shelter by a frustrated owner. So all of the "homework" you do in preparation for your pup's arrival will benefit you both. The more informed you are, the more you will know what to expect and the better equipped you will be to handle the ups and downs of raising a puppy. Hopefully, everyone in the household is willing to do his part in raising and caring for the pup. The anticipation of owning a dog often brings a lot of promises from excited family members: "I will walk him every day," "I will feed him," "I will house-train him," etc., but these things take time and effort, and promises can easily be forgotten once the novelty of the new pet has worn off.

PREPARING PUPPY'S PLACE IN YOUR HOME

Researching your breed and finding a breeder are only two aspects of the homework you will have to do before taking your Rat Terrier puppy home. You will also have to prepare your home and family for the new addition. Much as you would prepare a nursery for a newborn baby, you will need to designate a place in your home that will be the puppy's own. How you prepare your home will depend on how much freedom the dog will be allowed. Whatever you decide, you must ensure that he has a place that he can "call his own."

When you bring your new puppy into your home, you are bringing him into what will become his home as well. Obviously, you did not buy a puppy so that he could take over your house, but in order for a puppy to grow into a stable, well-adjusted dog, he has to feel comfortable in his surroundings. Remember, he is leaving the warmth and security of his mother and littermates, as well as the familiarity of the only place he has ever known, so it is important to make his transition as easy as possible. By preparing a place in your home for the puppy, you are making him feel as welcome as possible in a strange new place. It should not take him long to get used to it, but the sudden shock of being transplanted is somewhat traumatic for a young pup. Imagine how a small child would feel in the same situation—that is how your puppy must be feeling. It is up to you to reassure him and to let him know, "Little fellow, you are going to like it here!"

WHAT YOU SHOULD BUY

CRATE

To someone unfamiliar with the use of crates in dog training, it may seem like punishment to shut a dog in a crate, but this is not the case at all. Although all breeders do not advocate crate training, more and more breeders and trainers are recommending crates as preferred tools for show puppies as well as pet puppies. Crates are not cruel—crates have many humane and highly effective uses in dog care and training. For example, crate training is a very popular and very successful house-training method. A crate can keep your dog safe during

Alert and intelligent, the Rat Terrier puppy is an irresistible bundle of excitement, fun and responsibility.

travel and, perhaps most importantly, a crate provides your dog with a place of his own in your home. It serves as a "doggie bedroom" of sorts—your Rat Terrier can curl up in his crate when he wants to sleep or when he just needs a break. Many dogs sleep in their crates overnight. With soft bedding and his favorite toy, a crate becomes a cozy pseudo-den for your dog. Like his ancestors, he too will seek out the comfort and retreat of a den—you just happen to be providing him with something a little more luxu-

---

PUPPY APPEARANCE
Your puppy should have a well-fed appearance but not a distended abdomen, which may indicate worms or incorrect feeding, or both. The body should be firm, with a solid feel. The skin of the abdomen should be pale pink and clean, without signs of scratching or rash.

Introduce your Rat Terrier to his crate as soon as you bring him home. He will soon regard this as his "special place" for recreation and rest.

rious than what his early ancestors enjoyed.

As far as purchasing a crate, the type that you buy is up to you. It will most likely be one of the two most popular types: wire or fiberglass. There are advantages and disadvantages to each type. For example, a wire crate is more open, allowing the air to flow through and affording the dog a view of what is going on around him, while a fiberglass crate is sturdier. Both can double as travel crates, providing protection for the dog. The size of the crate is

Your local pet shop will have a large variety of crates from which you may choose the one which best suits your needs. The fiberglass is much sturdier and usually can last the lifetime of the dog.

PHOTO COURTESY OF DOSKOCIL.

CRATE-TRAINING TIPS

During crate training, you should partition off the section of the crate in which the pup stays. If he is given too big an area, this will hinder your training efforts. Crate training is based on the fact that a dog does not like to soil his sleeping quarters, so it is ineffective to keep a pup in an areathat is so big that he can eliminate in one end and get far enough away from it to sleep. Also, you want to make the crate den-like for the pup. Blankets and a favorite toy will make the crate cozy for the small pup; as he grows, you may want to evict some of his "roommates" to make more room. It will take some coaxing at first, but be patient. Given some time to get used to it, your pup will adapt to his new home-within-a-home quite nicely.

another thing to consider. Puppies do not stay puppies forever—in fact, sometimes it seems as if they grow right before your eyes. A small crate may be fine for a very young Rat Terrier pup, but it will not do him much good for long! Unless you have the money and the inclination to buy a new crate every time your pup has a growth spurt, it is better to get one that will accommodate your dog both as a pup and at full size. Depending on the size of your Rat Terrier, you will have to select a crate that will be large enough to

Take your time getting to know your new charge. Your Rat Terrier will soon be regarding you as his closest pal!

allow the adult dog to stand up and stretch out without any discomfort.

BEDDING

A lamb's wool crate pad in the dog's crate will help the dog feel more at home. This will take the place of the leaves, twigs, etc., that the pup would use in the wild to make a den; the pup can make his own "burrow" in the crate. Although your pup is far removed from his den-making ancestors, the denning instinct is still a part of his genetic makeup. Second, until you take your pup home, he has been sleeping amid the warmth of his dam and litter-mates, and while a blanket is not the same as a warm, breathing body, it still provides heat and something with which to snuggle. You will want to wash your pup's bedding frequently in case he has an accident in his crate, and replace or remove any crate pad or blanket that becomes ragged and starts to fall apart.

TOYS

Toys are a must for dogs of all ages, especially for curious playful pups. Puppies are the children of the dog world, and what child does not love toys? Chew toys provide enjoyment for both dog and owner—your dog will enjoy playing with his favorite toys, while you will enjoy the fact that they distract him from your expensive shoes and leather sofa. Puppies love to chew; in fact, chewing is a physical need for pups as they are teething, and everything looks appetizing! The full range of your possessions—from your favorite slipper to your new Persian carpet—are fair game in the eyes of a teething pup. Puppies are not all that discerning when it comes to finding some-thing to literally "sink their teeth into"—everything tastes great!

As youngsters they are often aggressive chewers, but they even-tually grow out of this. Puppies should be offered safe, sturdy

> ### A HEALTHY PUP
> You should not even think about buying a puppy that looks sick, under-nourished, overly frightened or nerv-ous. Sometimes a timid puppy will warm up to you after a 30-minute "let's-get-acquainted" session.

bones. Hide chews are also suitable. Always take care when giving squeaky toys, for Rat Terriers will usually remove squeaks and eyes immediately! This goes directly to their ratting instincts (and squeaking and squealing go hand in hand!). If a pup "disembowels" one of these, the small plastic squeaker inside can be dangerous if swallowed. Monitor the condition of all of your pup's toys carefully and get rid of any that have been chewed to the point of becoming potentially dangerous.

Adult Rat Terriers can be dedicated chewers so only the safest toys should be offered to them. Breeders advise owners to resist stuffed toys, because they can become de-stuffed in no time. The overly excited pup may ingest the stuffing, which is neither digestible nor nutritious.

Be careful of natural bones, which have a tendency to splinter into sharp, dangerous pieces. Also be careful of rawhide, which can turn into pieces that are easy to swallow and become a mushy mess on your carpet.

LEASH

A nylon leash is probably the best option as it is the most resistant to puppy teeth should your pup take a liking to chewing on his lead. Of course, this is a habit that should be nipped in the bud, but if your pup likes to chew on his lead he

TOYS, TOYS, TOYS!

With a big variety of dog toys available, and so many that look like they would be a lot of fun for a dog, be careful in your selection. It is amazing what a set of puppy teeth can do to an innocent-looking toy, so, obviously, safety is a major consideration. Be sure to choose the most durable products that you can find. Hard nylon bones and toys are a safe bet, and many of them are offered in different scents and flavors that will be sure to capture your dog's attention. It is always fun to play a game of fetch with your dog, and there are balls and flying discs that are specially made to withstand dog teeth.

has a very slim chance of being able to chew through the strong nylon. Nylon leads are also lightweight, which is good for a young Rat Terrier who is just getting used to the idea of walking on a lead. For everyday walking and safety purposes, the nylon lead is a good choice. As your pup grows up and gets used to walking on the lead, you may want to purchase a flexible lead. These leads allow you to extend the length to give the dog a broader area to explore or to shorten the length to keep the dog near you.

COLLAR

Your pup should get used to wearing a collar all the time since you will want to attach his ID tags to it. You have to attach the lead to something! A lightweight nylon collar is a good choice; make sure that it fits snugly enough so that the pup cannot wriggle out of it, but is loose enough so that it will not be uncomfortably tight around the pup's neck. You should be able to fit a finger between the pup and the collar. It may take some time for your pup to get used to wearing the collar, but soon he will not even notice that it is there. Choke collars are made for training, but should only be used by an experienced handler. The chain-type choke collars are not recommended for the Rat Terrier.

FOOD AND WATER BOWLS

Your pup will need two bowls, one for food and one for water. You may want two sets of bowls, one for inside and one for outside, depending on where the dog will be fed and where he will be

---

PET INSURANCE

Just as you can insure your car, your house and your own health, you likewise can insure your dog's health. Investigate a pet insurance policy by talking to your vet. Depending on the age of your dog, the breed and the kind of coverage you desire, your policy can be very affordable. Most policies cover accidental injuries, poisoning, and thousands of medical problems and illnesses, including cancers. Some carriers also offer routine care and immunization coverage.

CHOOSE AN APPROPRIATE COLLAR

The **BUCKLE COLLAR** is the standard collar used for everyday purposes. Be sure that you adjust the buckle on growing puppies. Check it every day. It can become too tight overnight! These collars can be made of leather or nylon. Attach your dog's identification tags to this collar.

The **CHOKE COLLAR** is designed for training. It is constructed of highly polished steel so that it slides easily through the stainless steel loop. The idea is that the dog controls the pressure around his neck and he will stop pulling if the collar becomes uncomfortable. It should *not* be used on a Rat Terrier.

The **HALTER** is for a trained dog that has to be restrained to prevent running away, chasing a cat and the like. Considered the most humane of all collars, it is frequently used on smaller dogs on which collars are not comfortable.

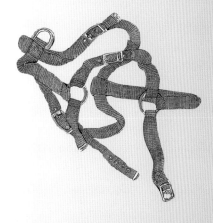

spending time. Stainless steel or sturdy plastic bowls are popular choices. Plastic bowls are more chewable. Dogs tend not to chew on the steel variety, which can be sterilized. It is important to buy sturdy bowls since anything is in danger of being chewed by puppy teeth and you do not want your dog to be constantly chewing apart his bowl (for his safety and for your purse!).

CLEANING SUPPLIES
Until a pup is house-trained, you will be doing a lot of cleaning. Accidents will occur, which is acceptable in the beginning because the puppy does not know any better. All you can do is be prepared to clean up any accidents. Old rags, towels, newspapers and a safe disinfectant are good to have on hand.

BEYOND THE BASICS
The items previously discussed are the bare necessities. You will find out what else you need as you go along—a dog brush and

PHOTO COURTESY OF MIKKI PET PRODUCTS.

comb, flea/tick protection, baby gates to partition a room, etc. These things will vary depending on your situation but it is important that you have everything you need to feed and make your Rat Terrier comfortable in his first few days at home.

PUPPY-PROOFING YOUR HOME

Aside from making sure that your Rat Terrier will be comfortable in your home, you also have to make sure that your home is safe for your Rat Terrier. This means taking precautions that your pup will not get into anything he should not get into and that there is nothing within his reach that may harm him should he sniff it, chew it, inspect it, etc. This probably seems obvious since, while you are primarily concerned with your pup's safety, at the same time you do not want your belongings to be ruined. Breakables should be placed out of reach if your dog is to have full run of the house. If he is to be limited to certain places within the house, keep any potentially dangerous items in the "off-limits" areas. An electrical cord can pose a danger should the puppy decide to taste it—and who is going to convince a pup that it would not make a great chew toy? Cords should be fastened tightly against the wall, out of the reach of the puppy. If your dog is going to spend time in a crate, make sure that there is nothing near his

NATURAL TOXINS

Examine your grass and landscaping before bringing your puppy home. Many varieties of plants have leaves, stems or flowers that are toxic if ingested, and you can depend on a curious puppy to investigate them.

If you see your dog carrying a piece of vegetation in his mouth, approach him in a quiet, disinterested manner, avoid eye contact, pet him and gradually remove the plant from his mouth. Alternatively, offer him a treat and maybe he'll drop the plant on his own accord. Be sure no toxic plants are growing in your own yard or kept in your home. Ask your vet for information on poisonous plants or research them at your library.

THE COCOA WARS

Chocolate contains the chemical thebromine, which is poisonous to dogs, although "chocolates" especially made for dogs are safe (as they don't actually contain chocolate) but not recommended. Any item that encourages your dog to enjoy the taste of cocoa should be discouraged. You should also exercise caution when using mulch in your garden. Many kinds of mulch frequently contain cocoa hulls, and dogs have been known to die from eating the mulch.

crate that he can reach if he sticks his curious little nose or paws through the openings. Just as you would with a child, keep all household cleaners and chemicals where the pup cannot reach them.

It is also important to make sure that the outside of your home is safe. Of course your puppy should never be unsupervised, but a pup let loose in the yard will want to run and explore, and he should be granted that freedom. Do not let a fence give you a false sense of security; you would be surprised how crafty (and persistent) a dog can be in working out how to dig under and squeeze his way through small holes, or to jump or climb over a fence. Rat Terriers are escape artists, and are quite gifted at digging deep holes in surprisingly short lengths of time. The remedy is to make the fence well embedded into the ground and high enough so that it really is impossible for your dog to get over it (about 6 feet should suffice). Be sure to repair or secure any gaps in the fence. Check the fence periodically to ensure that it is in good shape and make repairs as needed; a very determined pup may return to the same spot to "work on it" until he is able to get through.

Use treats to bribe your dog into a desired behavior. Try small pieces of hard cheese or freeze-dried liver.

FIRST TRIP TO THE VET

You have selected your puppy, and your home and family are ready. Now all you have to do is collect your Rat Terrier from the breeder and the fun begins, right? Well...not so fast. Something else you need to prepare is your pup's first trip to the vet. Perhaps the breeder can recommend someone in the area who specializes in terriers or small dog, or maybe you know some other Rat Terrier owners who can suggest a good vet. Either way, you should have an appointment arranged for your pup before you pick him up.

The pup's first visit will consist of an overall examination to make sure that the pup does not have any problems that are not apparent to you. The vet will also set up a schedule for the pup's vaccinations; the breeder will inform you of which ones the pup has already received and the vet can continue from there.

INTRODUCTION TO THE FAMILY

Everyone in the house will be excited about the puppy's coming home and will want to pet him and play with him, but it is best to make the introduction low-key so as not to overwhelm the puppy. He is apprehensive already. It is the first time he has been separated from his dam and the breeder, and the ride to your home is likely to be the first time he has been in a car. The last thing you want to do is smother him, as this will only frighten him further. This is not to say that human contact is not extremely necessary at this stage, because this is the time when a connection between the pup and his human family is formed. Gentle petting and soothing words should help console him, as well as just putting him down and letting him explore on his own (under your watchful eye, of course).

The pup may approach the family members or may busy himself with exploring for a while. Gradually, each person should spend some time with the pup, one at a time, crouching down to get as close to the pup's level as possible and letting him

HOW VACCINES WORK

If you've just bought a puppy, you surely know the importance of having your pup vaccinated, but do you understand how vaccines work? Vaccines contain the same bacteria or viruses that cause the disease you want to prevent, but they have been chemically modified so that they don't cause any harm. Instead, the vaccine causes your dog to produce antibodies that fight the harmful bacteria. Thus, if your dog is exposed to the disease in the future, the antibodies will destroy the viruses or bacteria.

sniff their hands and petting him gently. He definitely needs human attention and he needs to be touched—this is how to form an immediate bond. Just remember that the pup is experiencing a lot of things for the first time, at the same time. There are new people, new noises, new smells and new things to investigate: so be gentle, be affectionate and be as comforting as you can be.

PUP'S FIRST NIGHT HOME

You have traveled home with your new charge safely in his crate or a friend or family member's lap. He's been to the vet for a thorough checkup; he's been weighed, his papers examined; perhaps he's even been vaccinated and wormed as well. He's met the family, including the excited children and the less-than-happy cat. He's explored his crate, his new bed, the yard and anywhere else

Don't overdo the treats when training your puppy. In no time, your Rat Terrier will begin to regard his lessons as an extra meal.

he's been permitted. He's eaten his first meal at home and relieved himself in the proper place. He's heard lots of new sounds, smelled new friends and seen more of the outside world than ever before.

It's puppy's first night and you are ready to say "Good night"— keep in mind that this is puppy's first night ever to be sleeping alone. His dam and littermates are no longer at paw's length and he's a bit scared, cold and lonely. Be reassuring to your new family member. This is not the time to spoil him and give in to his inevitable whining.

Puppies whine. They whine to let others know where they are and hopefully to get company out of it. Place your pup in his new bed or crate in his room and close the door. Mercifully, he may fall asleep without a peep. When the inevitable occurs, ignore the whining: he is fine. Be strong and keep his interest in mind. Do not allow yourself to feel guilty and visit the pup. He will fall asleep eventually.

Many breeders recommend placing a piece of bedding from his former home in his new bed so that he recognizes the scent of his littermates. Others still advise placing a hot water bottle in his bed for warmth. This latter may be a good idea provided the pup doesn't attempt to suckle—he'll get good and wet and may not fall asleep so fast.

Puppy's first night can be somewhat stressful for the pup and his new family. Remember that you are setting the tone of nighttime at your house. Unless you want to play with your pup every night at 10 p.m., midnight and 2 a.m., don't initiate the habit. Your family will thank you, and so will your pup!

PREVENTING PUPPY PROBLEMS

SOCIALIZATION

Now that you have done all of the preparatory work and have helped your pup get accustomed to his new home and family, it is about time for you to have some fun! Socializing your Rat Terrier pup gives you the opportunity to show off your new friend, and your pup gets to reap the benefits of being

PROPER SOCIALIZATION
The socialization period for puppies is from age 8 to 16 weeks. This is the time when puppies need to leave their birth family and take up residence with their new owners, where they will meet many new people, other pets, etc. Failure to be adequately socialized can cause the dog to grow up fearing others and being shy and unfriendly due to a lack of self-confidence.

an adorable furry creature that people will want to pet and, in general, think is absolutely precious!

Besides getting to know his new family, your puppy should be exposed to other people, animals and situations, but of course he must not come into close contact with dogs you don't know well until his course of injections is fully complete. This will help him become well adjusted as he grows up and less prone to being timid

PUP MEETS WORLD

Thorough socialization includes not only meeting new people but also being introduced to new experiences such as riding in the car, having his coat brushed, hearing the television, walking in a crowd—the list is endless. The more your pup experiences, and the more positive the experiences are, the less of a shock and the less frightening it will be for your pup to encounter new things.

or fearful of the new things he will encounter. Your pup's socialization began with the breeder but now it is your responsibility to continue it. The socialization he receives up until the age of 12 weeks is the most critical, as this is the time when he forms his impressions of the outside world. Be especially careful during the eight-to-ten-week period, also known as the fear period. The interaction he receives during this time should be gentle and reassuring. Lack of socialization can manifest itself in fear and aggression as the dog grows up. He needs lots of human contact, affection, handling and exposure to other animals.

Once your pup has received his necessary vaccinations, feel free to take him out and about (on his lead, of course). Walk him around the neighborhood, take him on your daily errands, let people pet him, let him meet other dogs and pets, etc. Puppies do not have to try to make friends; there will be no shortage of people who will want to introduce themselves. Just make sure that you carefully supervise each meeting. If the neighborhood children want to say hello, for example, that is great—children and pups most often make great companions. Sometimes an excited child can unintentionally handle a pup too roughly, or an overzealous pup can playfully nip a little too hard. You want to make socialization experiences positive ones. What a pup learns during this very formative stage will affect his attitude toward future encounters. You want your dog to be comfortable around everyone. A pup that has a bad experience with a child may grow up to be a dog that is shy around or aggressive toward children.

CONSISTENCY IN TRAINING
Dogs, being pack animals, naturally need a leader, or else they try to establish dominance in their packs. When you welcome a dog into your family, the choice of who becomes the leader and who becomes the pack is entirely up to you! Your pup's intuitive quest for dominance, coupled with the fact that it is nearly impossible to look at an adorable Rat Terrier pup

with his puppy-dog eyes and button nose and not cave in, give the pup almost an unfair advantage in getting the upper hand! A pup will definitely test the waters to see what he can and cannot do. Do not give in to those pleading eyes—stand your ground when it comes to disciplining the pup and make sure that all family members do the same. It will only confuse the pup when Mother tells him to get off the sofa when he is used to sitting up there with Father to watch the nightly news. Avoid discrepancies by having all members of the household decide on the rules before the pup even comes home…and be consistent in enforcing them! Early training shapes the Rat Terrier's behavior and personality, so you cannot be unclear in what you expect of the puppy.

CHEWING TIPS

Chewing goes hand in hand with nipping in the sense that a teething puppy is always looking for a way to soothe his aching gums. In this case, instead of chewing on you, he may have taken a liking to your favorite shoe or something else that he should not be chewing. Again, realize that this is a normal canine behavior that does not need to be discouraged, only redirected. Your pup just needs to be taught what is acceptable to chew on and what is off-limits. Consistently tell him "No!" when you catch him chewing on something forbidden and give him a chew toy.

Conversely, praise him when you catch him chewing on something appropriate. In this way, you are discouraging the inappropriate behavior and reinforcing the desired behavior. The puppy's chewing should stop after his adult teeth have come in, but an adult dog continues to chew for various reasons—perhaps because he is bored, needs to relieve tension or just likes to chew. That is why it is important to redirect his chewing when he is still young.

COMMON PUPPY PROBLEMS

The best way to prevent puppy problems is to be proactive in stopping an undesirable behavior as soon as it starts. The old saying "You can't teach an old dog new tricks" does not necessarily hold true, but it is true that it is much easier to discourage bad behavior in a young developing pup than to wait until the pup's bad behavior becomes the adult dog's bad habit. There are some problems that are especially prevalent in puppies as they develop.

NIPPING

As puppies start to teethe, they feel the need to sink their teeth into anything available...unfortunately that includes your fingers, arms, hair and toes. You may find this behavior cute for the first five seconds...until you feel just how sharp those puppy teeth are. This is something you want to discourage immediately and consistently with a firm "No!" (or whatever number of firm "Nos" it takes for him to understand that you mean business). Then replace your finger with an appropriate chew toy. While this behavior is merely annoying when the dog is young, it can become dangerous as your Rat Terrier's adult teeth grow in and his jaws develop, and he continues to think it is okay to gnaw on human appendages. Your Rat Terrier does not mean any harm with a friendly nip, but he

---

IN DUE TIME

It will take at least two weeks for your puppy to become accustomed to his new surroundings. Give him lots of love, attention, handling, frequent opportunities to relieve himself, a diet he likes to eat and a place he can call his own.

---

also does not know the strength of his own rat-killing jaw bones.

CRYING/WHINING

Your pup will often cry, whine, whimper, howl or make some type of commotion when he is left alone. This is basically his way of calling out for attention to make sure that you know he is there and that you have not forgotten about him. He feels insecure when he is left alone, when you are out of the house and he is in his crate or when you are in another part of the house and he cannot see you. The noise he is making is an expression of the anxiety he feels at being alone, so he needs to be taught that being alone is okay. You are not actually training the dog to stop making noise, you are training him to feel comfortable when he is alone and thus removing the need for him to make the noise. This is where the crate with cozy bedding and a toy comes in handy. You want to know that he is safe when you are not there to supervise, and you know that he

Keep your Rat Terrier puppy occupied with safe chew toys in a stimulating environment and you will minimize the problems that can accompany ownership.

will be safe in his crate rather than roaming freely about the house. In order for the pup to stay in his crate without making a fuss, he needs to be comfortable in his crate. On that note, it is extremely important that the crate is never used as a form of punishment, or the pup will have a negative association with the crate.

Accustom the pup to the crate in short, gradually increasing time intervals in which you put him in the crate, maybe with a treat, and stay in the room with him. If he cries or makes a fuss, do not go to him, but stay in his sight. Gradually he will realize that staying in his crate is okay without your help, and it will not be so traumatic for him when you are not around. You may want to leave the radio on softly when you leave the house; the sound of human voices may be comforting to him.

RAT TERRIER

FEEDING THE RAT TERRIER
When you first bring your Rat Terrier puppy home, the breeder will encourage you to continue feeding the dog what he has been fed up to then. Any changes to diet should be made gradually to avoid upsetting the puppy's digestion. Up to about four months old, your Rat Terrier will need about four meals a day. Feedings can then be reduced to three, and then, two, at around eight months. Adult Rat Terriers normally thrive on one meal a day, with a few daily hard biscuits to keep the teeth clean.

Be cautious and watch for allergies in your Rat Terrier puppy. Some dogs cannot tolerate eggs, which is not really a problem, since the adult dog may enjoy but will not require dairy products.

With today's variety of nutritionally complete foods, choosing what to feed your Rat Terrier should depend on what keeps your dog fit and what works best for you. Balance is the key and should include proteins, carbohydrates, vitamins and minerals, the latter two are already found in many prepared dog foods. The Rat Terrier will, of course, be happy to vary his diet with fish, eggs and cheese. While most have a healthy appetite, you may find

STORING DOG FOOD
You must store your dry dog food carefully. Open packages of dog food quickly lose their vitamin value, usually within 90 days of being opened. Mold spores and vermin could also contaminate the food.

yourself with a finicky eater and a little resourcefulness on your part will be required. Patient trial and error to find his favorites will usually solve the dilemma, as well as trying feedings at different times.

Some terrier breeders encourage owners to supplement their dogs' diets with vitamin B. Brewers' yeast tablets, a good source of vitamin B, are easily available, and breeders find this supplement good for the nerves and quite beneficial to high-strung, anxious terriers. Vitamin E is also recommended for keeping the coat in good, healthy, shiny condition.

DIETARY AND FEEDING CONSIDERATIONS

Dog foods are produced in three basic types: dry, semi-moist and canned. Dry foods are useful for the cost-conscious for overall they tend to be less expensive than semi-moist or canned. They also contain the least fat and the most preservatives. In general, canned foods are made up of 60–70% water, while semi-moist ones often contain so much sugar that they are perhaps the least preferred by owners, even though their dogs seem to like them. When selecting your dog's diet, three stages of development must be considered: the puppy stage, the adult stage and the senior stage.

FEEDING TIPS
- Dog food must be served at room temperature, neither too hot nor too cold. Fresh water, changed often and served in a clean bowl, is mandatory, especially when feeding dry food.
- Never feed your dog from the table while you are eating, and never feed your dog leftovers from your own meal. They usually contain too much fat and too much seasoning.
- Dogs must chew their food. Hard pellets are excellent; soups and stews are to be avoided.
- Don't add leftovers or any extras to commercial dog food. The normal food is usually balanced, and adding something extra destroys the balance.
- Except for age-related changes, dogs do not require dietary variations. They can be fed the same diet, day after day, without theirbecoming bored or ill.

The breeder allows the puppies to nurse from their dam for the first six weeks, assessing the weight gain of each puppy as he develops. If a puppy is not gaining weight steadily, the breeder may choose to supplement feedings.

PUPPY STAGE

Puppies instinctively want to suck milk from their mother's teats and a normal puppy will exhibit this behavior from just a few moments following birth. If puppies do not attempt to suckle within the first half-hour or so, they should be encouraged to do so by placing them on the nipples, having selected ones with plenty of milk. This early milk supply is important in providing colostrum to protect the puppies during the first eight to ten weeks of their

lives. Although a mother's milk is much better than any milk formula, despite there being some excellent ones available, if the puppies do not feed, the breeder will have to feed them himself. For those with less experience, advice from a vet is important so that you feed not only the right quantity of milk but that of correct quality, fed at suitably frequent intervals, usually every two hours

THE CANINE GOURMET

Your dog does not prefer a fresh bone. Indeed, he wants it properly aged and, if given such a treat indoors, he is more likely to try to bury it in the carpet than he is to settle in for a good chew! If you have a garden, give him such delicacies outside and guide him to a place suitable for his "bone yard." He will carefully place the treasure in its earthy vault and seemingly forget about it. Trust me, his seeming distaste or lack of thanks for your thoughtfulness is not that at all. He will return in a few days to inspect the bone, perhaps to re-bury it, and when it is just right, he will relish it as much as you do that cooked-to-perfection steak. If he is in a concrete or bricked kennel run, he will be especially frustrated at the hopelessness of the situation. He will vacillate between ignoring it completely, giving it a few licks to speed the curing process with saliva, and trying to hide it behind the water bowl! When the bone has aged a bit, he will set to work on it.

during the first few days of life.

Puppies should be allowed to nurse from their dam for about the first six weeks, although from the third or fourth week the breeder begins to introduce small portions of suitable solid food. Most breeders like to introduce alternate milk and meat meals initially, building up to weaning time.

By the time the puppies are seven or a maximum of eight weeks old, they should be fully weaned and fed solely on a proprietary puppy food. Selection of the most suitable, good-quality diet at this time is essential, for a puppy's fastest growth rate is during the first year of life. Vets are usually able to offer advice in this regard and, although the frequency of meals will have been reduced over time, only when a young dog has reached the age of about four months should an adult diet be fed. Rat Terriers continue to develop physically until they are three years of age. Puppy and junior diets should be well balanced for the needs of your dog, so that except in certain circumstances additional vitamins, minerals and proteins will not be required.

ADULT DIETS

A dog is considered an adult when he has stopped growing, so in general the diet of a Rat Terrier can be changed to an adult one at about four months of age. Again

FOOD PREFERENCE

Selecting the best dry dog food is difficult. There is no majority consensus among veterinary scientists as to the value of nutrient analysis (protein, fat, fiber, moisture, ash, cholesterol, minerals, etc.). All agree that feeding trials are what matter most, but you also have to consider the individual dog. The dog's weight, age and activity level, and what pleases his taste, all must be considered. It is probably best to take the advice of your veterinarian. Every dog has individual dietary requirements, and should be fed accordingly.

If your dog is fed a good dry food, he does not require supplements of meat or vegetables. Dogs do appreciate a little variety in their diets, so you may choose to stay with the same brand but vary the flavor. Alternatively, you may wish to add a little flavored stock to give a difference to the taste.

Ideally you will continue feeding your puppy the same diet that the breeder began. Changes in a puppy's diet should take gradually or else you can upset the dog's digestion process.

you should rely upon your vet or dietary specialist to recommend an acceptable maintenance diet. Major dog-food manufacturers specialize in this type of food, and it is merely necessary for you to select the one best suited to your dog's needs. Active dogs may have different requirements than sedate dogs.

SENIOR DIETS

As dogs get older, their metabolisms change. The older dog usually exercises less, moves more slowly and sleeps more. This change in lifestyle and physiological performance requires a change in diet. Since these changes take place slowly, they might not be recognizable. What is easily recognizable is weight gain. By continuing to feed your dog an adult-maintenance diet when he is slowing down metabolically, your dog will gain weight. Obesity in an older dog compounds the health problems that already accompany old age.

As your dog gets older, few of his organs function up to par. The kidneys slow down and the intestines become less efficient. These age-related factors are best handled with a change in diet and a change in feeding schedule to give smaller portions that are more easily digested.

There is no single best diet for every older dog. While many dogs do well on light or senior diets, other dogs do better on puppy diets or other special premium diets such as lamb and rice. Be sensitive to your senior Rat Terrier's diet and this will help control other problems that may arise with your old friend.

WATER

Just as your dog needs proper nutrition from his food, water is an essential nutrient as well. Water keeps the dog's body properly hydrated and promotes normal function of the body's systems. During housebreaking it is necessary to keep an eye on how much water your Rat Terrier is drinking, but once he is reliably trained he should have access to clean fresh water at all times, especially if you feed dry food.

TEST FOR PROPER DIET

A good test for proper diet is the color, odor and firmness of your dog's stool. A healthy dog usually produces three semi-hard stools per day. The stools should have no unpleasant odor. They should be the same color from excretion to excretion.

Make certain that the dog's water bowl is clean, and change the water often.

EXERCISE FOR YOUR RAT TERRIER

While the Rat Terrier will proudly bolt a rabbit or rid you of a rat, he is primarily a companion dog and will be equally as happy to stroll around the yard with his family. Still, he is an active, hardy little fellow and you will bring out his best with a sufficient amount of exercise.

The breed adapts well to life indoors or out, city or rural. If you live in the country, your Rat Terrier will dazzle you with his curiosity and stamina. He will race through bush and bramble, over walls and across fields, exuberant and eager to explore. Don't, however, allow him off-lead until you are certain he is responsive to commands. And, as with any dog off-lead, do make sure he has an identification tag.

The Rat Terrier in the suburbs, in a fenced-off run, should not be allowed to laze around without any exercise. Being outdoors does not compensate for a couple of good walks a day on his lead. A nice walk through the neighborhood will stimulate his terrier inquisitiveness and keep him happier and fit!

The same should be encouraged for the city apartment dweller. The Rat Terrier thrives on

GRAIN-BASED DIETS

Some less expensive dog foods are based on grains and other plant proteins. While these products may appear to be attractively priced, many breeders prefer a diet based on animal proteins and believe that they are more conducive to your dog's health. Many grain-based diets rely on soy protein, which may cause flatulence (passing gas).

There are many cases, however, when your dog might require a special diet. These special requirements should only be recommended by your veterinarian.

regular walks, and whether on city streets or in parks, he will love these opportunities to explore and socialize. If your area has a dog run, where he is safe from escape or injury, do let him off the lead to enjoy a good scamper and scramble.

For those with interest and energy, kennel and breed clubs

DRINK, DRANK, DRUNK— MAKE IT A DOUBLE

In both humans and dogs, as well as other living organisms, water forms the major part of nearly every body tissue. Naturally, we take water for granted, but without it, life as we know it would cease.

For dogs, water is needed to keep their bodies functioning biochemically. Additionally, water is needed to replace the water lost while panting. Unlike humans, who are able to sweat to dissipate heat, dogs must pant to cool down, thereby losing the vital water that their bodies need to regulate their body temperatures. Humans lose electrolyte-containing products and other body-fluid components through sweating; dogs do not lose anything except water.

Water is essential always, but especially so when the weather is hot or humid or when your dog is exercising or working vigorously.

host special events where Rat Terriers compete against each other in conformation, agility, obedience, rat racing and going to ground (earthdog events). With the breed's love to please, many really excel in agility. You and your Rat Terrier will both be well exercised after these events! Keep your Rat Terrier fit in mind and body and you will be rewarded with a happy and self-fulfilled companion.

GROOMING YOUR RAT TERRIER

With his sleek, beautiful, natural "wash and wear" appearance, the coated Rat Terrier is a low-maintenance companion, requiring only periodic baths, brushing, nail trimming and teeth cleaning. The Hairless variety, which will be discussed below, has its own grooming routine to stay healthy, but is almost as "care-free" as its Coated cousins.

The Coated Rat Terrier does shed and this will require regular brushing with a soft brush or rubber curry mitt to remove dead hair. The breed's shedding season is normally heavier in the spring and fall, or after seasonal heat cycles or whelping. (In very cold climates, Rat Terriers that are outdoors a lot may develop a thicker coat.) A simple daily brushing is recommended, though a real good grooming once a week will keep your Rat Terrier's coat

The Rat Terrier has a short coat and requires very little in the way of grooming, other than regular brushing to minimize shedding.

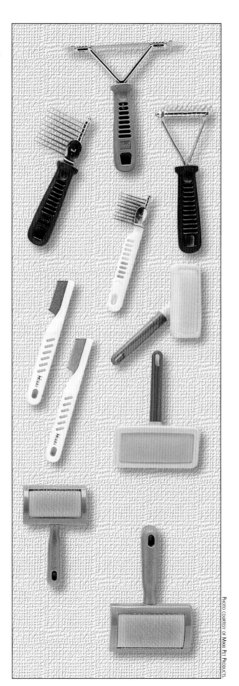

GROOMING EQUIPMENT

Invest in quality grooming tools that will last you and your Rat Terrier for many years of use. Here are some basics:

- Bristle brush
- Grooming glove
- Metal comb
- Rubber mat
- Dog shampoo
- Spray hose attachment
- Towels
- Ear cleaner
- Cotton balls
- Nail clippers and file
- Dental-care products

in prime condition. It will also give you the opportunity to examine your dog for any ear, eye or skin problems. Many dogs look forward to their grooming routine. If you accustom your Rat Terrier to being brushed and handled, he will come to see the experience as fun, an opportunity to spend time with you. If your dog seems a bit hesitant or feisty at first, try alternating a little massage along with the brushing, or give him an occasional treat as you groom. Within a human family, keeping a youngster clean and healthy expresses a parent's love and concern for the child. It is the same for your dog. Your Rat Terrier will appreciate the care you show him and see the experience as an expression of your love. Don't be surprised if he soon races over to you when you get out his brush!

As with any other breed, an occasional bath, with a good rinse, cleaning of the anal glands and periodic nail trims will keep your Rat Terrier in good shape. Talk to your dog, assuring him whenever you work on sensitive areas. Some breeders use bluing or brighteners on the white markings, but watch out for hives. If you take your Rat Terrier to a professional groomer, remind them to "leave the whiskers." Whiskers are a natural part of your dog's look and are an aid to him as Nature intended them to be.

The Hairless variety, with its soft, smooth skin, is very easy to keep clean and needs only routine attention to be protected and feel good. Like Coated dogs, they produce a normal amount of lubricating skin oil and can be bathed normally. While their skin is quite durable, do be aware that like any exposed skin, it is very susceptible to sunburn, so, if outdoors, apply sun lock to your hairless Rat Terrier or protect him with clothing. Once covered, your dog is very similar to his Coated counterparts in his tolerance to weather, although like many breeds, the Rat Terrier prefers the cold to the heat and humidity. Fans of the Hairless are quick to assure prospective owners that a

Hairless is every bit as vigorous as his tough little brethren in coats!

Some call the Rat Terrier a "self-cleaning" little dog. Those with coat shed dirt, and both types are odor-free. With good nutrition and a simple grooming routine, the breed stays fit, smart looking and full of himself! Keeping your Rat Terrier in prime condition takes a minimum of time. But the bond you build reaps a maximum of love and loyalty.

BATHING

Dogs do not need to be bathed as often as humans, but regular bathing is essential for healthy

A summer shower al fresco, is one way to bathe your Rat Terrier.

BATHING BEAUTY

Once you are sure that the dog is thoroughly rinsed, squeeze the excess water out of his coat with your hand and dry him with an heavy towel. You may choose to use a blow dryer on his coat or just let it dry naturally. In cold weather, never allow your dog outside with a wet coat.

There are "dry bath" products on the market, which are sprays and powders intended for spot cleaning, that can be used between regular baths if necessary. They are not substitutes for regular baths, but they are easy to use for touch-ups as they do not require rinsing.

skin and a healthy, shiny coat. Again, like most anything, if you accustom your pup to being bathed as a puppy, it will be second nature by the time he grows up. You want your dog to be at ease in the bath or else it could end up a wet, soapy, messy ordeal for both of you!

Brush your Rat Terrier thoroughly before wetting his coat. This will get rid of most mats and tangles, which are harder to remove when the coat is wet. Make certain that your dog has a good non-slip surface to stand on. Begin by wetting the dog's coat. A shower or hose attachment is necessary for thoroughly wetting and rinsing the coat. Check the water temperature to make sure that it is neither too hot nor too cold.

Next, apply shampoo to the dog's coat and work it into a good lather. You should purchase a shampoo that is made for dogs. Do not use a product made for human hair. Wash the head last; you do not want shampoo to drip into the dog's eyes while you are washing the rest of his body. Work the shampoo all the way down to the skin. You can use this opportunity to check the skin for any bumps, bites or other abnormalities. Do not neglect any area of the body—get all of the hard-to-reach places.

Once the dog has been thoroughly shampooed, he requires an equally thorough rinsing.

A slicker brush over the coat on a daily basis will only take a minute or two, and your Rat Terrier will enjoy the quality time spent together.

Nail Clipping

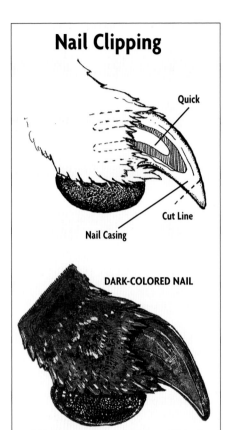

Quick

Cut Line

Nail Casing

DARK-COLORED NAIL

With black nails, it's best to clip only a small bit of the nail at a time or to use a file where the quick is not visible.

LIGHT-COLORED NAIL

In light-colored nails, clipping is much simpler because you can see the vein (or quick) that grows inside the nail casing.

Clean the outer ear with a soft wipe and ear cleanser. Never probe into the ear canal.

Shampoo left in the coat can be irritating to the skin. Protect his eyes from the shampoo by shielding them with your hand and directing the flow of water in the opposite direction. You should also avoid getting water in the ear canal. Once bathed, many Rat Terriers find it great fun to streak around the home, leaping from couch to rug, rolling and rubbing to assist in the drying process. Stand back and enjoy the entertainment!

EAR CARE

It is always necessary to keep a dog's ears clean, and this is especially important in the case of a Rat Terrier that has such large ears. Ears should be kept clean using a special cleaner, but take care not to delve too deeply into the ear canal as this might cause injury.

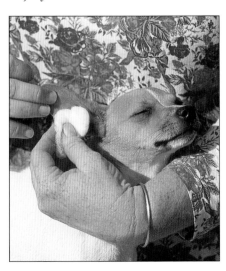

NAILS

Never forget that toenails should be kept short. How frequently the nails will need to be clipped will depend on how much a dog walks on hard surfaces, but they should be checked on a weekly basis. Canine nail clippers can easily be obtained from pet shops, and many owners find those of the guillotine design easier to use. A nail file can also be used to give a good finish to the nails. However, it is important to introduce a Rat Terrier to routine nail care from an early age, for many can be very awkward about this.

TEETH

Teeth should always be kept as free from tartar as possible. There are now several canine tooth-cleaning agents available, includ-ing the basics, like a small tooth-brush and canine toothpaste.

TRAVELING WITH YOUR DOG

CAR TRAVEL

You should accustom your Rat Terrier to riding in a car at an early age. You may or may not take him in the car often, but at the very least he will need to go to the vet and you do not want these trips to be traumatic for the

> **PEDICURE TIP**
>
> A dog that spends a lot of time outside on a hard surface, such as cement or pavement, will have his nails naturally worn down and may not need to have them trimmed as often, except maybe in the colder months when he is not outside as much. Regardless, it is best to get your dog accustomed to the nail-trimming procedure at an early age so that he is used to it. Some dogs are especially sensitive about having their feet touched, but if a dog has experienced it since puppyhood, it should not bother him.

Yes, we brush our Rat Terriers' teeth regularly. Accustom the young dog to this procedure, and you will have no problem being your dog's dental hygienist!

Your local pet shop will have special clippers for maintaining short nails on your Rat Terrier.

Inspect your dog's teeth on a regular basis. The teeth should be white and clean, the gums pink and the breath fresh!

dog or troublesome for you. The safest way for a dog to ride in the car is in his crate. If he uses a crate in the house, you can use the same crate for travel.

Put the pup in the crate and see how he reacts. If he seems uneasy, you can have a passenger hold him on his lap while you drive. Another option is a specially made safety harness for dogs, which straps the dog in much like a seat belt. Do not let the dog roam loose in the car—this is very dangerous! If you should stop short, your dog can be thrown and injured. If the dog starts climbing on you and pestering you while you are driving, you will not be able to concentrate on the road. It is an unsafe situation for everyone—human and canine.

For long trips, be prepared to stop to let the dog relieve himself. Take with you whatever you need to clean up after him, including some paper towels and perhaps some old towels for use should he have an accident in the car or suffer from motion sickness.

AIR TRAVEL

Contact your chosen airline before proceeding with your travel plans that include your Rat Terrier. The dog will be required to travel in a fiberglass crate and you should always check in advance with the airline regarding specific requirements for the crate's size, type and labeling. To help put the dog at ease, give him one of his favorite toys in the crate. Do not feed the dog for several hours prior to checking in so that you minimize his need to relieve himself. However, some airlines require that the dog must be fed within four hours of arriving at the airport, in which case a light meal is best. For long trips, you will have to attach food and water bowls to the dog's crate so that airline employees can tend to him between legs of the trip.

Make sure your dog is properly identified and that your contact information appears on his ID tags and on his crate. Animals travel in a different area of the plane than human passen-

ON THE ROAD

If you are going on a long motor trip with your dog, be sure the hotels are dog-friendly. Many hotels do not accept dogs. Also take along some ice that can be thawed and offered to your dog if he becomes overheated. Most dogs like to lick ice.

TRAVEL ALERT

When you travel with your dog, it's a good idea to take along water from home or to buy bottled water for the trip. In areas where water is sometimes chemically treated and sometimes comes right out of the ground, you can prevent adverse reactions to this essential part of your dog's diet.

members of the family. You would probably make arrangements for accommodations ahead of time anyway, but this is especially important when traveling with a dog. You do not want to make an overnight stop at the only place around for miles and find out that they do not allow dogs. Also, you do not want to reserve a place for your family without confirming that you are traveling with a dog because if it is against their policy you may not have a place to stay.

Alternatively, if you are traveling and choose not to bring your Rat Terrier, you will have to make arrangements for him while you are away. Some options are to take him to a neighbor's house to stay while you are gone, to have a

gers so every rule must be strictly adhered to so as to prevent the risk of getting separated from your dog.

BOARDING

So you want to take a family trip—and you want to include all

Although your Rat Terriers look stylish cruising in the front seat of your sedan, they must be safely confined to their crates whenever traveling. This is the safest possible method of traveling with any dog.

trusted neighbor stop by often or stay at your house, or bring your dog to a reputable boarding kennel. If you choose to board him at a kennel, you should visit in advance to see the facilities provided, how clean they are and

LET THE SUN SHINE
Your dog needs daily sunshine for the same reason people do. Pets kept inside homes with curtains drawn against the sun suffer from "SAD" (Seasonal Affected Disorder) to the same degree as humans. We now know that sunlight must enter the iris and thus progress to the pineal gland to regulate the body's hormonal system. When we live and work in artificial light, both circadian rhythms and hormone balances are disturbed.

where the dogs are kept. Talk to some of the employees and see how they treat the dogs—do they spend time with the dogs, play with them, exercise them, etc.? Also find out the kennel's policy on vaccinations and what they require. This is for all of the dogs' safety, since when dogs are kept together, there is a greater risk of diseases being passed from dog to dog.

IDENTIFICATION
Your Rat Terrier is your valued companion and friend. That is why you always keep a close eye on him and you have made sure that he cannot escape from the yard or wriggle out of his collar and run away from you. However,

accidents can happen and there may come a time when your dog unexpectedly gets separated from you. If this unfortunate event should occur, the first thing on your mind will be finding him. Proper identification, including an ID tag, a tattoo, and possibly a microchip, will increase the chances of his being returned to you safely and quickly.

IDENTIFICATION OPTIONS

As puppies become more and more expensive, especially those puppies of high quality for showing and/or breeding, they have a greater chance of being stolen. The usual collar dog tag is, of course, easily removed. But there are two more permanent techniques that have become widely used for identification.

The puppy microchip implantation involves the injection of a small microchip, about the size of a corn kernel, under the skin of the dog. If your dog shows up at a clinic or shelter, or is offered for resale under less-than-savory circumstances, it can be positively identified by the microchip. The microchip is scanned, and a registry quickly identifies you as the owner.

Tattooing is done on various parts of the dog, from his belly to his ears. The number tattooed can be your telephone number, your dog's registration number or any other number that you can easily memorize. When professional dog thieves see a tattooed dog, they usually lose interest. For the safety of our dogs, no laboratory facility or dog broker will accept a tattooed dog as stock.

Discuss microchipping and tattooing with your veterinarian and breeder. Some vets perform these services on their own premises for a reasonable fee. To ensure that your dog's identification is effective, be certain that the dog is then properly registered with a legitimate national database.

Select a boarding kennel based upon cost, convenience and the approval of your vet.

Your Rat Terrier must always wear a light collar to which is attached his identification tag.

TRAINING YOUR

RAT TERRIER

Living with an untrained dog is a lot like owning a piano that you do not know how to play—it is a nice object to look at but it does not do much more than that to bring you pleasure. Now try taking piano lessons and suddenly the piano comes alive and brings forth magical sounds and rhythms that set your heart singing and your body swaying.

The same is true with your Rat Terrier. Any dog is a big responsibility and if not trained sensibly may develop unacceptable behavior that annoys you or could even cause family friction.

To train your Rat Terrier, you may want to enroll in an obedience class. Teach him good manners as you learn how and why he behaves the way he does. Find out how to communicate with your dog and how to recognize and understand his communications with you. Suddenly the dog takes on a new role in your life—he is clever, interesting, well-behaved and fun to be with. He demonstrates his bond of devotion to you daily. In other words, your Rat Terrier does wonders for your ego because he constantly reminds you that you

FEAR AGGRESSION

Pups who are subjected to physical abuse during training commonly end up with behavioral problems as adults. One common result of abuse is fear aggression, in which a dog will lash out, bare his teeth, snarl and finally bite someone by whom he feels threatened. For example, your daughter may be playing with the dog one afternoon. As they play hide-and-seek, she backs the dog into a corner and, as she attempts to tease him playfully, he bites her hand. Examine the cause of this behavior. Did your daughter ever hit the dog? Did someone who resembles your daughter hit or scream at the dog?

Fortunately, fear aggression is relatively easy to correct. Have your daughter engage in only positive activities with the dog, such as feeding, petting and walking. She should not give any corrections or negative feedback. If the dog still growls or cowers away from her, allow someone else to accompany them. After approximately one week, the dog should feel that he can rely on her for many positive things, and he will also be prevented from reacting fearfully towards anyone who might resemble her.

SAFETY FIRST

While it may seem that the most important things to your dog are eating, sleeping and chewing the upholstery on your furniture, his first concern is actually safety. The domesticated dogs we keep as companions have the same pack instinct as their ancestors who ran free thousands of years ago. Because of this pack instinct, your dog wants to know that he and his pack are not in danger of being harmed, and that his pack has a strong, capable leader. You must establish yourself as the leader early on in your relationship. That way your dog will trust that you will take care of him and the pack, and he will accept your commands without question.

tial. Unfortunately, many owners of untrained adult dogs lack the patience factor, so they do not persist until their dogs are successful at learning particular behaviors.

Training a puppy aged 10 to 16 weeks (20 weeks at the most) is like working with a dry sponge in a pool of water. The pup soaks up whatever you show him and constantly looks for more things to do and learn. At this early age, his body is not yet producing hormones, and therein lies the reason for such a high rate of success. Without hormones, he is focused on his owners and not particularly interested in investigating other places, dogs, people, etc. You are his leader: his

are not only his leader, you are his hero!

Those involved with teaching dog obedience and counseling owners about their dogs' behavior have discovered some interesting facts about dog ownership. For example, training dogs when they are puppies results in the highest rate of success in developing well-mannered and well-adjusted adult dogs. Training an older dog, from six months to six years of age, can produce almost equal results providing that the owner accepts the dog's slower rate of learning capability and is willing to work patiently to help the dog succeed at developing to his fullest poten-

A young puppy is a dry sponge waiting to be soaked by his teacher. Douse your Rat Terrier puppy with fun lessons and lots of love and praise.

PARENTAL GUIDANCE

Training a dog is a life experience. Many parents admit that much of what they know about raising children they learned from caring for their dogs. Dogs respond to love, fairness and guidance, just as children do. Become a good dog owner and you may become an even better parent.

provider of food, water, shelter and security. He latches onto you and wants to stay close. He will usually follow you from room to room, will not let you out of his sight when you are outdoors with him and will respond in like manner to the people and animals you encounter. If you greet a friend warmly, he will be happy to greet the person as well. If, however, you are hesitant, even anxious, about the approach of a stranger, your dog will respond accordingly.

Once the puppy begins to produce hormones, his natural curiosity emerges and he begins to investigate the world around him. It is at this time when you may notice that the untrained dog begins to wander away from you and even ignore your commands to stay close. When this behavior becomes a problem, the owner has two choices: get rid of the dog or train him. It is strongly urged that you choose the latter option.

There are usually classes within a reasonable distance from the owner's home, but you can also do a lot to train your dog yourself. Sometimes there are classes available but the tuition is too costly. Whatever the circumstances, the solution to the problem of training your Rat Terrier without formal obedience classes lies within the pages of this book. This chapter is devoted to helping you train your Rat Terrier at home.

If the recommended procedures are followed faithfully, you may expect positive results that will prove rewarding both to you and your dog.

Whether your new charge is a puppy or a mature adult, the methods of teaching and the techniques we use in training basic behaviors are the same. After all, no dog, whether puppy or adult, likes harsh or inhumane methods. All creatures, however, respond favorably to gentle motivational methods and sincere praise and encouragement. Now let us get started.

HOUSE-TRAINING

You can train a puppy to relieve himself wherever you choose, but this must be somewhere suitable. You should bear in mind from the outset that when your puppy is old enough to go out in public places, any canine droppings must be removed at once. You will always have to carry with you a small plastic bag or "poop-scoop."

Outdoor training includes such surfaces as grass, soil and cement. Indoor training usually means training your dog to newspaper. When deciding on the surface and location that you will want your Rat Terrier to use, be sure it is going to be permanent. Training your dog to grass and then changing your mind two months later is extremely difficult

REAP THE REWARDS
If you start with a normal, healthy dog and give him time, patience and some carefully executed lessons, you will reap the rewards of that training for the life of the dog. And what a life it will be! The two of you will find immeasurable pleasure in the companionship you have built together with love, respect and understanding.

for both dog and owner.

Next, choose the command you will use each and every time you want your puppy to void. "Hurry up" and "Potty" are examples of commands commonly used by dog owners.

Get in the habit of giving the puppy your chosen relief command before you take him out. That way, when he becomes

CANINE DEVELOPMENT SCHEDULE

It is important to understand how and at what age a puppy develops into adulthood. If you are a puppy owner, consult the following Canine Development Schedule to determine the stage of development your puppy is currently experiencing. This knowledge will help you as you work with the puppy in the weeks and months ahead.

Period	Age	Characteristics
FIRST TO THIRD	BIRTH TO SEVEN WEEKS	Puppy needs food, sleep and warmth, and responds to simple and gentle touching. Needs mother for security and disciplining. Needs littermates for learning and interacting with other dogs. Pup learns to function within a pack and learns pack order of dominance. Begin socializing pup with adults and children for short periods. Pup begins to become aware of his environment.
FOURTH	EIGHT TO TWELVE WEEKS	Brain is fully developed. Needs socializing with outside world. Remove from mother and littermates. Needs to change from canine pack to human pack. Human dominance necessary. Fear period occurs between 8 and 12 weeks. Avoid fright and pain.
FIFTH	THIRTEEN TO SIXTEEN WEEKS	Training and formal obedience should begin. Less association with other dogs, more with people, places, situations. Period will pass easily if you remember this is pup's change-to-adolescence time. Be firm and fair. Flight instinct prominent. Permissiveness and over-disciplining can do permanent damage. Praise for good behavior.
JUVENILE	FOUR TO EIGHT MONTHS	Another fear period about 7 to 8 months of age. It passes quickly, but be cautious of fright and pain. Sexual maturity reached. Dominant traits established. Dog should understand sit, down, come and stay by now.

NOTE: THESE ARE APPROXIMATE TIME FRAMES. ALLOW FOR INDIVIDUAL DIFFERENCES IN PUPPIES.

an adult, you will be able to determine if he wants to go out when you ask him. A confirmation will be signs of interest, such as wagging his tail, watching you intently, going to the door, etc.

PUPPY'S NEEDS

The puppy needs to relieve himself after play periods, after each meal, after he has been sleeping and at any time he indicates that he is looking for a place to urinate or defecate. The urinary and intestinal tract muscles of very young puppies are not fully developed. Therefore, like human babies, puppies need to relieve themselves frequently.

Take your puppy out often—every hour for an eight week old, for example, and always immediately after sleeping and eating. The older the puppy, the less often he will need to relieve himself. Finally, as a mature healthy adult, he will require only three to five relief trips per day.

HOUSING

Since the types of housing and control you provide for your puppy have a direct relationship on the success of house-training, we consider the various aspects of both before we begin training. Taking a new puppy home and turning him loose in your house can be compared to turning a child loose in a sports arena and telling the child that the place is

Make the puppy feel a part of your family right from the beginning. This youngster awaits a long career as a show dog and companion.

all his! The sheer enormity of the place would be too much for him to handle.

Instead, offer the puppy clearly defined areas where he can play, sleep, eat and live. A room of the house where the family gathers is the most obvious choice. Puppies are social animals and need to feel a part of the pack right from the start. Hearing your voice, watching you while you are doing things and smelling you nearby are all positive reinforcers that he is now a member of your pack. Usually a family room, the kitchen or a nearby adjoining breakfast area is ideal for providing safety and security for both puppy and owner.

Within that room there should be a smaller area that the puppy can call his own. An alcove, a wire or fiberglass dog crate or a gated corner from which he can view the activities of his new family will be fine. The size of the area or crate is the key factor here. The area must be large enough for the puppy to lie down and stretch out as well as stand up without rubbing his head on the top, yet

THE SUCCESS METHOD

Success that comes by luck is usually short-lived. Success that comes by well-thought-out proven methods is often more easily achieved and permanent. This is the Success Method. It is designed to give you, the puppy owner, a simple yet proven way to help your puppy develop clean living habits and a feeling of security in his new environment.

6 Steps to Successful Crate Training

1 Tell the puppy "Crate time!" and place him in the crate with a small treat (a piece of cheese or half of a biscuit). Let him stay in the crate for five minutes while you are in the same room. Then release him and praise lavishly. Never release him when he is fussing. Wait until he is quiet before you let him out.

2 Repeat Step 1 several times a day.

3 The next day, place the puppy in the crate as before. Let him stay there for ten minutes. Do this several times.

4 Continue building time in five-minute increments until the puppy stays in his crate for 30 minutes with you in the room. Always take him to his relief area after prolonged periods in his crate.

5 Now go back to Step 1 and let the puppy stay in his crate for five minutes, this time while you are out of the room.

6 Once again, build crate time in five-minute increments with you out of the room. When the puppy will stay willingly in his crate (he may even fall asleep!) for 30 minutes with you out of the room, he will be ready to stay in it for several hours at a time.

HOW MANY TIMES A DAY?

AGE	RELIEF TRIPS
To 14 weeks	10
14–22 weeks	8
22–32 weeks	6
Adulthood	4
(dog stops growing)	

These are estimates, of course, but they are a guide to the *minimum* number of opportunities a dog should have each day to relieve himself.

small enough so that he cannot relieve himself at one end and sleep at the other without coming into contact with his droppings until fully trained to relieve himself outside. The designated area should contain clean bedding and a toy. Water must always be available, in a non-spill container.

Dogs are, by nature, clean animals and will not remain close to their relief areas unless forced to do so. In those cases, they then become dirty dogs and usually remain that way for life.

CONTROL

By *control*, we mean helping the puppy to create a lifestyle pattern that will be compatible to that of his human pack (you). Just as we guide little children to learn our way of life, we must show the puppy when it is time to play, eat, sleep, exercise and even entertain himself.

Your puppy should always sleep in his crate. He should also learn that, during times of household confusion and excessive human activity such as at breakfast when family members are preparing for the day, he can play by himself in relative safety and comfort in his designated area. Each time you leave the puppy alone, he should understand exactly where he is to stay. Puppies are chewers. They cannot tell the difference between lamp cords, television wires, shoes, table legs, etc. Chewing into a television wire, for example, can be fatal to the puppy while a shorted wire can start a fire in the house.

If the puppy chews on the arm of the chair when he is alone, you will probably discipline him

To begin a lesson, be sure that you have the puppy's undivided attention. Sometimes a flea can really interrupt valuable lesson plans.

PRACTICE MAKES PERFECT!

- Have training lessons with your dog every day in several short segments—three to five times a day for a few minutes at a time is ideal.
- Do not have long practice sessions. The dog will become easily bored.
- Never practice when you are tired, ill, worried or in an otherwise negative mood. This will transmit to the dog and may have an adverse effect on his performance.

  Think fun, short and above all *positive!* End each session on a high note, rather than a failed exercise, and make sure to give a lot of praise. Enjoy the training and help your dog enjoy it, too.

angrily when you get home. Thus, he makes the association that your coming home means he is going to be punished. (He will not remember chewing the chair and is incapable of making the association of the discipline with his naughty deed.)

Other times of excitement, such as holidays, family parties, etc., can be fun for the puppy providing he can view the activities from the security of his designated area. He is not underfoot and he is not being fed all sorts of tidbits that will probably cause him stomach distress, yet he still feels a part of the fun.

SCHEDULE

A puppy should be taken to his relief area each time he is released from his designated area, after meals, after a play session and when he first awakens in the morning (at age eight weeks, this can mean 5 a.m.!). The puppy will indicate that he's ready "to go" by circling or sniffing busily—do not misinterpret these signs. For a puppy less than ten weeks of age, a routine of taking him out every hour is necessary. As the puppy grows, he will be able to wait for longer periods of time.

Keep trips to his relief area short. Stay no more than five or six minutes and then return to the house. If he goes during that time, praise him lavishly and take him indoors immediately. If he does

TRAINING RULES

If you want to be successful in training your dog, you have four rules to obey yourself:

1. Develop an understanding of how a dog thinks.
2. Do not blame the dog for lack of communication.
3. Define your dog's personality and act accordingly.
4. Have patience and be consistent.

versus the times for relief. Help him develop regular hours for naps, being alone, playing by himself and just resting, all in his crate. Encourage him to entertain himself while you are busy with your activities. Let him learn that having you near is comforting, but it is not your main purpose in life to provide him with undivided attention.

Each time you put a puppy in his own area, use the same command, whatever suits best. Soon he will run to his crate or special area when he hears you say those words.

Crate training provides safety for you, the puppy and the home. It also provides the puppy with a feeling of security, and that helps the puppy achieve self-confidence and clean habits. Remember that

not, but he has an accident when you go back indoors, pick him up immediately, say "No! No!" and return to his relief area. Wait a few minutes, then return to the house again. Never hit a puppy or rub his face in urine or excrement when he has had an accident!

Once indoors, put the puppy in his crate until you have had time to clean up his accident. Then release him to the family area and watch him more closely than before. Chances are, his accident was a result of your not picking up his signal or waiting too long before offering him the opportunity to relieve himself. Never hold a grudge against the puppy for accidents.

Let the puppy learn that going outdoors means it is time to relieve himself, not play. Once trained, he will be able to play indoors and out and still differentiate between the times for play

Your puppy will learn that a visit to the yard does not always mean it's time to play. Structure is key to training any puppy.

one of the primary ingredients in house-training your puppy is control. Regardless of your lifestyle, there will always be occasions when you will need to have a place where your dog can stay and be happy and safe. Crate training is the answer for now and in the future.

In conclusion, a few key elements are really all you need for a successful house-training method—consistency, frequency, praise, control and supervision. By following these procedures with a normal, healthy puppy, you and the puppy will soon be past the stage of "accidents" and ready to move on to a full and rewarding life together.

ROLES OF DISCIPLINE, REWARD AND PUNISHMENT

Discipline, training one to act in accordance with rules, brings order to life. It is as simple as that. Without discipline, particularly in a group society, chaos reigns supreme and the group will eventually perish. Humans and canines are social animals and need some form of discipline in order to function effectively. They must procure food, protect their home base and their young and reproduce to keep the species going.

If there were no discipline in the lives of social animals, they would eventually die from starvation and/or predation by other

HOUSE-TRAINING TIP

Most of all, be consistent. Always take your dog to the same location, always use the same command and always have the dog on lead when he is in his relief area, unless a fenced-in yard is available.

By following the Success Method, your puppy will be completely house-broken by the time his muscle and brain development reach maturity. Keep in mind that small breeds usually mature faster than large breeds, but all puppies should be trained by six months of age.

stronger animals. In the case of domestic canines, dogs need discipline in their lives in order to understand how their pack (you and other family members) functions and how they must act in order to survive.

A large humane society in a highly populated area recently surveyed dog owners regarding their satisfaction with their relationships with their dogs. People who had trained their dogs were 75% more satisfied with their pets than those who had never trained their dogs.

Dr. Edward Thorndike, a noted psychologist, established Thorndike's Theory of Learning, which states that a behavior that results in a pleasant event tends to be repeated. Likewise, a behavior that results in an unpleasant event tends not to be repeated. It is this theory on which training methods are based today. For example, if you manipulate a dog to perform a specific behavior and reward him for doing it, he is likely to do it again because he enjoyed the end result.

Occasionally, punishment, a penalty inflicted for an offense, is necessary. The best type of punishment often comes from an outside source. For example, a child is told not to touch the stove because he may get burned. He disobeys and touches the stove. In doing so, he receives a burn. From that time on, he respects the heat

THE STUDENT'S STRESS TEST

During training sessions, you must be able to recognize signs of stress in your dog such as:
- tucking his tail between his legs
- lowering his head
- shivering or trembling
- standing completely still or running away
- panting and/or salivating
- avoiding eye contact
- flattening his ears back
- urinating submissively
- rolling over and lifting a leg
- grinning or baring teeth
- aggression when restrained

If your four-legged student displays these signs, he may just be nervous or intimidated. The training session may have been too lengthy, with not enough praise and affirmation. Stop for the day and try again tomorrow.

of the stove and avoids contact with it. Therefore, a behavior that results in an unpleasant event tends not to be repeated.

A good example of a dog learning the hard way is the dog who chases the housecat. He is told many times to leave the cat alone, yet he persists in teasing the cat. Then, one day he begins chasing the cat but the cat turns and swipes a claw across the dog's face, leaving him with a painful gash on his nose. The final result is that the dog stops chasing the cat.

TRAINING EQUIPMENT

COLLAR AND LEAD
For a Rat Terrier the collar and lead that you use for training must be one with which you are easily able to work, not too heavy for the dog and perfectly safe.

TREATS
Have a bag of treats on hand. Something nutritious and easy to swallow works best. Use a soft treat, a chunk of cheese or a piece of cooked chicken rather than a dry biscuit. By the time the dog has finished chewing a dry treat, he will forget why he is being rewarded in the first place! Using food rewards will not teach a dog to beg at the table—the only way to teach a dog to beg at the table is to give him food from the table. In training, rewarding the dog with a

CALM DOWN
Dogs will do anything for your attention. If you reward the dog when he is calm and attentive, you will develop a well-mannered dog. If, on the other hand, you greet your dog excitedly and encourage him to wrestle with you, the dog will greet you the same way and you will have a hyperactive dog on your hands.

COMMAND STANCE

Stand up straight and authoritatively when giving your dog commands. Do not issue commands when lying on the floor or lying on your back on the sofa. If you are on your hands and knees when you give a command, your dog will think you are positioning yourself to play.

food treat will help him associate praise and the treats with learning new behaviors that obviously please his owner.

TRAINING BEGINS: ASK THE DOG A QUESTION

In order to teach your dog anything, you must first get his attention. After all, he cannot learn anything if he is looking away from you with his mind on something else. To get his attention, ask him "School?" and immediately walk over to him and give him a treat as you tell him "Good dog." Wait a minute or two and repeat the routine, this time with a treat in your hand as you approach within a foot of the dog. Do not go directly to him, but stop about a foot short of him and hold out the treat as you ask "School?" He will see you approaching with a treat in your hand and most likely begin walking toward you. As you meet, give him the treat and praise again.

The third time, ask the ques-

tion, have a treat in your hand and walk only a short distance toward the dog so that he must walk almost all the way to you. As he reaches you, give him the treat and praise again.

By this time, the dog will probably be getting the idea that if he pays attention to you, especially when you ask that question, it will pay off in treats and enjoyable activities for him. In other words, he learns that "school" means doing great things with you that are fun and result in positive attention for him.

Keep the dog's focus while practicing with the training lead. "School" should be a fun and rewarding time.

The sit command is the ideal place to start when training your dog. Practice this lesson every day and use it to keep every lesson ending on a positive (successful) note.

Remember that the dog does not understand your verbal language; he only recognizes sounds. Your question translates to a series of sounds for him, and those sounds become the signal to go to you and pay attention; if he does, he will get to interact with you plus receive treats and praise.

THE BASIC COMMANDS

TEACHING SIT

Now that you have the dog's attention, attach his lead and hold it in your left hand and a food treat in your right. Place your food hand at the dog's nose and let him lick the treat but not take it from you. Say "Sit" and slowly raise your food hand from in front of the dog's nose up over his head so that he is looking at the ceiling. As he bends his head upward, he will have to bend his knees to maintain his balance. As he bends his knees, he will assume a sit position. At that point, release the food treat and praise lavishly with comments such as "Good dog! Good sit!" Remember to always praise enthusiastically, because dogs relish verbal praise from their owners and feel so proud of themselves whenever they accomplish a behavior.

You will not use food forever in getting the dog to obey your commands. Food is only used to teach new behaviors, and once the dog knows what you want when you give a specific command, you will wean him off the food treats but still maintain the verbal praise. After all, you will always have your voice with you, and there will be many times when you have no food rewards but expect the dog to obey.

TEACHING DOWN

Teaching the down exercise is easy when you understand how the dog perceives the down position, and it is very difficult when you do not. Dogs perceive the down position as a submissive one, therefore teaching the down exercise using a forceful method can sometimes make the dog develop such a fear of the down that he either runs away when you say "Down" or he attempts to snap at the person who tries to force him down.

Have the dog sit close alongside your left leg, facing in the same direction as you are. Hold the lead in your left hand and a food treat in your right. Now place your left hand lightly on the top of the dog's shoulders where they meet above the spinal cord. Do not push down on the dog's shoulders; simply rest your left hand there so you can guide the dog to lie down close to your left leg rather than to swing away from your side when he drops.

Now place the food hand at the dog's nose, say "Down" very softly (almost a whisper), and slowly lower the food hand to the dog's front feet. When the food hand reaches the floor, begin moving it forward along the floor in front of the dog. Keep talking softly to the dog, saying things like, "Do you want this treat? You can do this, good dog." Your reassuring tone of voice will help calm the dog as he tries to follow the food hand in order to get the treat.

When the dog's elbows touch

DOUBLE JEOPARDY

A dog in jeopardy never lies down. He stays alert on his feet because instinct tells him that he may have to run away or fight for his survival. Therefore, if a dog feels threatened or anxious, he will not lie down. Consequently, it is important to keep the dog calm and relaxed as he learns the down exercise.

the floor, release the food and praise softly. Try to get the dog to maintain that down position for several seconds before you let him sit up again. The goal here is to get the dog to settle down and not feel threatened in the down position.

TEACHING STAY

It is easy to teach the dog to stay in either a sit or a down position. Again, we use food and praise during the teaching process as we help the dog to understand exactly what it is that we are expecting him to do.

To teach the sit/stay, start with the dog sitting on your left side as before and hold the lead in your left hand. Have a food treat in your right hand and place your food hand at the dog's nose. Say "Stay" and step out on your right foot to stand directly in front of the dog, toe to toe, as he licks and nibbles the treat. Be sure to keep his head facing upward to maintain the sit position. Count to five and then swing around to stand next to the dog again with him on your left. As soon as you get back to the original position, release the food and praise lavishly.

To teach the down/stay, do the down as previously described. As soon as the dog lies down, say "Stay" and step out on your right foot just as you did in the sit/stay. Count to five and then return to stand beside the dog with him on your left side. Release the treat and praise as always.

Within a week or ten days, you can begin to add a bit of distance between you and your dog when you leave him. When you do, use your left hand open with the palm facing the dog as a stay signal, much the same as the hand signal a police officer uses to stop traffic at an intersection. Hold the food treat in your right hand as before, but this time the food is not touching the dog's nose. He will watch the food hand and quickly learn that he is going to get that treat as soon as you return to his side.

When you can stand 1 yard away from your dog for 30 seconds, you can then begin building time and distance in both stays. Eventually, the dog can be expected to remain in the stay position for prolonged periods of time until you return to him or call him to you. Always praise lavishly when he stays.

"WHERE ARE YOU?"

When calling the dog, do not say "Come." Say things like, "Rover, where are you? See if you can find me! I have a biscuit for you!" Keep up a constant line of chatter with coaxing sounds and frequent questions such as, "Where are you?" The dog will learn to follow the sound of your voice to locate you and receive his reward.

TEACHING COME

If you make teaching "come" a fun experience, you should never have a student that does not love the game or that fails to come when called. The secret, it seems, is never to teach the word "come." At times when an owner most wants his dog to come when called, the owner is likely to be upset or anxious and he allows these feelings to come through in the tone of his voice when he calls his dog. Hearing that desperation in his owner's voice, the dog fears the results of going to him and therefore either disobeys outright or runs in the opposite direction. The secret, therefore, is to teach the dog a game and, when you want him to come to you, simply play the game. It is

Practice the down command in a variety of environs once the dog gets used to what's expected of him.

practically a no-fail solution!

To begin, have several members of your family take a few food treats and each go into a different room in the house. Take turns calling the dog, and each

"COME" . . . BACK

Never call your dog to come to you for a correction or scold him when he reaches you. That is the quickest way to turn a come command into "Go away fast!" Dogs think only in the present tense, and your dog will connect the scolding with coming to you, not with the misbehavior of a few moments earlier.

person should celebrate the dog's finding him with a treat and lots of happy praise. When a person calls the dog, he is actually inviting the dog to find him and get a treat as a reward for "winning."

A few turns of the "Where are you?" game and the dog will understand that everyone is playing the game and that each person has a big celebration awaiting his success at locating them. Once he learns to love the game, simply calling out "Where are you?" will bring him running from wherever he is when he hears that all-important question.

The come command is recognized as one of the most important things to teach a dog, but there are trainers who work with thousands of dogs and never teach the actual word "come." Yet these dogs will race to respond to a person who uses the dog's name followed by "Where are you?" For example, a woman has a 12-year-old companion dog who went blind, but who never fails to locate her owner when asked, "Where are you?'

Children, in particular, love to play this game with their dogs. Children can hide in smaller places like a shower stall or bathtub, behind a bed or under a table. The dog needs to work a little bit harder to find these hiding places, but when he does he loves to celebrate with a treat and a tussle with a favorite youngster.

TEACHING HEEL

Heeling means that the dog walks beside the owner without pulling. It takes time and patience on the owner's part to succeed at teaching the dog that he (the owner) will not proceed unless the dog is walking calmly beside him. Pulling out ahead on the lead is definitely not acceptable.

Begin by holding the lead in your left hand as the dog sits beside your left leg. Move the loop end of the lead to your right hand but keep your left hand short on the lead so it keeps the dog in close next to you. Say "Heel" and step forward on your left foot. Keep the dog close to you and take three steps. Stop and have the dog sit next to you in what we now call the heel position. Praise verbally, but do not touch the dog. Hesitate a moment and begin again with "Heel," taking three steps and stopping, at which point the dog is told to sit again.

Your goal here is to have the dog walk those three steps without pulling on the lead. Once he will walk calmly beside you for three steps without pulling, increase the number of steps you take to five. When he will walk politely beside you while you take five steps, you can increase the length of your walk to ten steps. Keep increasing the length of your stroll until the dog will walk quietly beside you without

TUG OF WALK?

If you begin teaching the heel by taking long walks and letting the dog pull you along, he misinterprets this action as an acceptable form of taking a walk. When you pull back on the leash to counteract his pulling, he reads that tug as a signal to pull even harder!

FETCH!
Play fetching games with your puppy in an enclosed area where he can retrieve his toy and bring it back to you. Always use a toy or object designated just for this purpose. Never use a shoe, sock or other item he may later confuse with those in your closet or underneath your chair.

exercise is finished and the dog is free to relax.

If you are dealing with a dog who insists on pulling you around, simply "put on your brakes" and stand your ground until the dog realizes that the two of you are not going anywhere until he is beside you and moving at your pace, not his. It may take some time just standing there to convince the dog that you are the leader and you will be the one to decide on the direction and speed of your travel.

Each time the dog looks up at you or slows down to give a slack lead between the two of you, quietly praise him and say, "Good heel. Good dog." Eventually, the dog will begin to respond and within a few days he will be walking politely beside you without pulling on the lead. At first, the training sessions should be kept short and very positive; soon the dog will be able to walk nicely with you for increasingly longer distances. Remember also to give the dog free time and the opportunity to run and play when you have finished heel practice.

WEANING OFF FOOD IN TRAINING
Food is used in training new behaviors. Once the dog understands what behavior goes with a specific command, it is time to start weaning him off the food treats. At first, give a treat after

pulling as long as you want him to heel. When you stop heeling, indicate to the dog that the exercise is over by verbally praising as you pet him and say "OK, good dog." The "OK" is used as a release word, meaning that the each exercise. Then, start to give a treat only after every other exercise. Mix up the times when you offer a food reward and the times when you only offer praise so that the dog will never know when he is going to receive both food and praise and when he is going to receive only praise. This is called a variable-ratio reward system and it proves successful because there is always the chance that the owner will produce a treat, so the dog never stops trying for that reward. No matter what, always give verbal praise.

OBEDIENCE CLASSES

It is a good idea to enroll in an obedience class if one is available in your area. If yours is a show dog, handling classes would be more appropriate. Many areas have dog clubs that offer basic obedience training as well as preparatory classes for obedience competition. There are also local dog trainers who offer similar classes.

At obedience trials, dogs can earn titles at various levels of competition. The beginning levels of competition include basic behaviors such as sit, down, heel, etc. The more advanced levels of competition include jumping, retrieving, scent discrimination and signal work. The advanced levels require a dog and owner to put a lot of time and effort into their training and the titles that

HOW TO WEAN THE "TREAT HOG"

If you have trained your dog by rewarding him with a treat each time he performs a command, he may soon decide that without the treat, he won't sit, stay or come. The best way to fix this problem is to start asking your dog to do certain commands twice before being rewarded. Slowly increase the number of commands given and then vary the number: three sits and a treat one day, five sits for a biscuit the next day, etc. Your dog will soon realize that there is no set number of sits before he gets his reward and he'll likely do it the first time you ask in the hope of being rewarded sooner rather than later.

Rat Terriers excel in many organized competitions, including obedience and agility. Here's Millie clearing the bar jump at an agility trial.

can be earned at these levels of competition are very prestigious.

OTHER ACTIVITIES FOR LIFE
Whether a dog is trained in the structured environment of a class or alone with his owner at home, there are many activities that can

bring fun and rewards to both owner and dog once they have mastered basic control.

Teaching the dog to help out around the home, in the yard or on the farm provides great satisfaction to both dog and owner. In addition, the dog's help makes life a little easier for his owner and raises his stature as a valued

Many Rat Terriers are trained to work on farms, as demonstrated by this rapid little Feist rounding up the ponies.

HELPING PAWS

Your dog may not be the next Lassie, but every pet has the potential to do some tricks well. Identify his natural talents and hone them. Is your dog always happy and upbeat? Teach him to wag his tail or give you his paw on command. Real homebodies can be trained to do household chores, such as carrying dirty laundry or retrieving the morning paper.

Through the hoop! Another fabulous performance by a talented Rat Terrier.

companion to his family. It helps give the dog a purpose by occupying his mind and providing an outlet for his energy.

If you are interested in participating in organized competition with your Rat Terrier, there are activities other than obedience in which you and your dog can become involved. Rat Terriers are working dogs and thrive when they are given an activity. The American Working Terrier Association, an affiliated club of the American Kennel Club, permits Rat Terriers to participate in earthdog trials. Even though the Rat Terrier is not a digging terrier like the Cairn or Scottie, he does have paws that are pretty good at digging (for certain!) and makes quite a go at these trials. The Rat Terriers cannot, however, earn Earthdog titles at present. The breed's hunting skills can also be employed for hunting. They are eager to chase anything

from mice to deer!

Agility is a popular sport where dogs run through an obstacle course that includes various jumps, tunnels and other exercises to test the dog's speed and coordination. The owners run beside their dogs to give commands and to guide them through the course. Although competitive, the focus is on fun—it's fun to do, fun to watch and great exercise. Rat Terriers, eager to please and impress, are excellent contenders in agility trials.

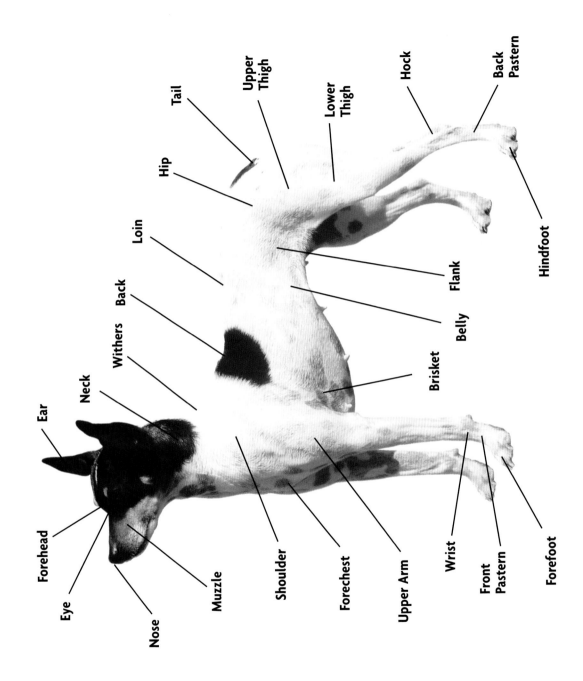

PHYSICAL STRUCTURE OF THE RAT TERRIER

RAT TERRIER

Dogs suffer from many of the same physical illnesses as people, including cancer, allergies, heart conditions, diabetes and many others. Since people usually know more about human diseases than canine maladies, many of the terms used in this chapter will be familiar but not necessarily those used by veterinarians. We will use the term *x-ray*, instead of the more acceptable term *radiograph*. We will also use the familiar term *symptoms* even though dogs don't have symptoms, which are verbal descriptions of the patient's feelings; dogs have *clinical signs*. Since dogs can't speak, we have to look for *clinical signs*...but we still use the term *symptoms* in this book.

As a general rule, medicine is practiced. That term is not arbitrary. Medicine is a constantly changing art as we learn more and more about genetics, electronic aids (like CAT scans and MRIs) and daily laboratory advances. There are many dog maladies, like canine hip dysplasia, which are not universally treated in the same manner. Some vets opt for surgery more often than others do.

SELECTING A VET

Your selection of a veterinarian should be based not only upon his ability with small dogs and his personality but also upon his convenience to your home. You want a vet who is close because you might have emergencies or need to make multiple visits for treatments. You want a vet who has services that you might require such as boarding, tattooing and grooming, as well as sophisticated pet supplies and a good reputation for ability and responsiveness. There is nothing more frustrating than having to wait a day or more to get a response from your vet.

All vets are licensed and their diplomas and/or certificates should be displayed in their waiting rooms. There are, however, many veterinary specialties that usually require further studies and internships. There are specialists in heart problems (veterinary cardiologists), skin problems (veterinary dermatologists), teeth and gum problems (veterinary dentists), eye problems (veterinary ophthalmologists) and x-rays (veterinary radiologists), as

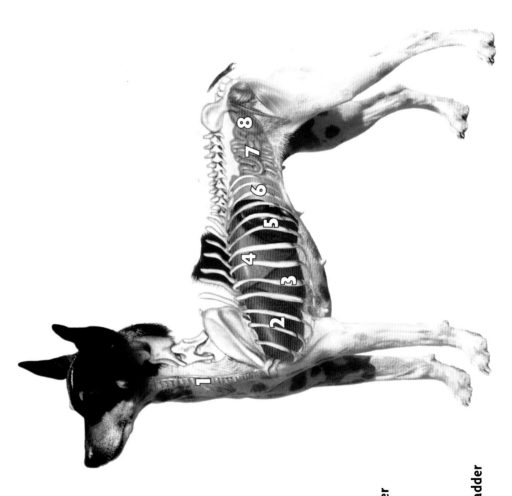

1. Esophagus
2. Lungs
3. Gall Bladder
4. Liver
5. Kidney
6. Stomach
7. Intestines
8. Urinary Bladder

INTERNAL ORGANS OF THE RAT TERRIER

well as vets who have specialties in bones, muscles or other organs. Most vets do routine surgery such as neutering, stitching up wounds and docking tails for those breeds in which such is required for show purposes. When the problem affecting your dog is serious, it is not unusual or impudent to get another medical opinion, although it is courteous to advise the vets concerned about this. You might also want to compare costs among several veterinarians. Sophisticated health care and veterinary services can be very costly. It is not infrequent that important decisions are based upon financial considerations.

PREVENTATIVE MEDICINE
It is much easier, less costly and more effective to practice preventative medicine than to fight bouts of illness and disease. Properly bred puppies come from parents who were selected based upon their genetic-disease profiles. Their dam should have been vaccinated, free of all internal and external parasites and properly nourished. For these reasons, a visit to the vet who cared for the dam is recommended. The dam can pass on disease resistance to her puppies, which can last for eight to ten weeks. She can also pass on parasites and many infections. That's why you should learn as much about the dam's health as possible.

Breakdown of Veterinary Income by Category

2%	Dentistry
4%	Radiology
12%	Surgery
15%	Vaccinations
19%	Laboratory
23%	Examinations
25%	Medicines

A typical vet's income, categorized according to services performed. This survey dealt with small-animal (pets) practices.

VACCINATION SCHEDULING
Most vaccinations are given by injection and should only be done by a vet. From the onset of your relationship with your vet, be sure to advise him that Rat Terriers can be particularly sensitive to inoculations and other injections. Both he and you should keep a record of the date of the injection, the identification of the vaccine and the amount given. Some vets give a first vaccination at eight weeks, but most dog breeders prefer the course not to commence until about ten weeks because of negating any antibodies passed on by the dam. The vaccination scheduling is usually based on a 15-day cycle. You must take your vet's advice regarding when to vaccinate as this may differ according to the vaccine used. Most vaccinations immunize your puppy against viruses.

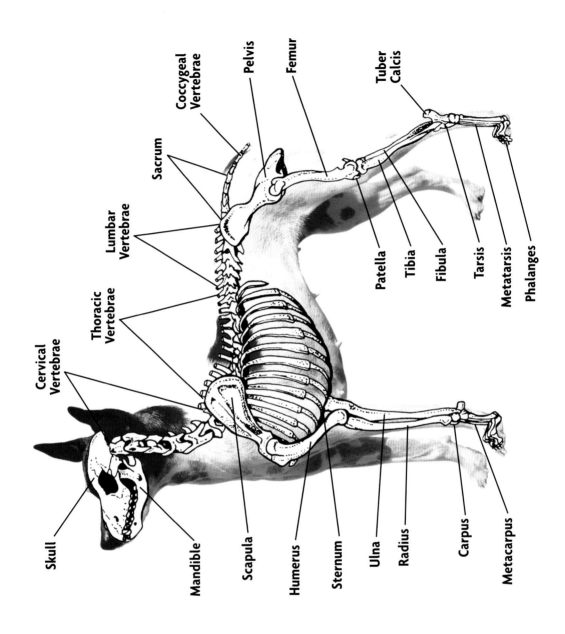

Coccygeal Vertebrae

Pelvis

Femur

Tuber Calcis

Sacrum

Lumbar Vertebrae

Patella

Tibia

Fibula

Tarsis

Metatarsis

Phalanges

Thoracic Vertebrae

Cervical Vertebrae

Skull

Mandible

Scapula

Humerus

Sternum

Ulna

Radius

Carpus

Metacarpus

SKELETAL STRUCTURE OF THE RAT TERRIER

The usual vaccines contain immunizing doses of several different viruses such as distemper, parvovirus, parainfluenza and hepatitis although some veterinarians recommend separate vaccines for each disease. There are other vaccines available when the puppy is at risk. You should rely upon professional advice. This is especially true for the booster-shot program. Most vaccination programs require a booster when the puppy is a year old and once a year thereafter. In some cases, circumstances may require more or less frequent immunizations. Canine cough, more formally known as tracheobronchitis, is treated with a vaccine that is sprayed into the dog's nostrils. Canine cough is usually included in routine vaccination, but this is often not so effective as for other major diseases.

WEANING TO FIVE MONTHS OLD
Puppies should be weaned by the time they are about two months old. A puppy that remains for at least eight weeks with his dam and littermates usually adapts better to other dogs and people later in life. Some new owners have their puppy examined by a

HEALTH AND VACCINATION SCHEDULE

AGE IN WEEKS:	6TH	8TH	10TH	12TH	14TH	16TH	20-24TH	52ND
Worm Control	✔	✔	✔	✔	✔	✔	✔	
Neutering							✔	
Heartworm		✔		✔		✔	✔	
Parvovirus	✔		✔		✔		✔	✔
Distemper		✔		✔		✔		✔
Hepatitis		✔		✔		✔		✔
Leptospirosis								✔
Parainfluenza	✔		✔		✔			✔
Dental Examination		✔					✔	✔
Complete Physical		✔					✔	✔
Coronavirus				✔			✔	✔
Canine Cough	✔							
Hip Dysplasia								✔
Rabies							✔	

Vaccinations are not instantly effective. It takes about two weeks for the dog's immune system to develop antibodies. Most vaccinations require annual booster shots. Your vet should guide you in this regard.

vet immediately, which is a good idea. Vaccination programs usually begin when the puppy is very young.

The puppy will have his teeth examined and have his skeletal conformation and general health checked prior to certification by the vet. Rat Terrier puppies can have problems with their kneecaps and undescended testicles; other common puppy problems include cataracts and other eye problems and heart murmurs. They may also have personality problems and your

vet might have training in temperament evaluation.

FIVE TO TWELVE MONTHS OF AGE
Unless you intend to breed or show your dog, neutering the puppy at six months of age is recommended. Discuss this with your vet. Neutering has proven to be extremely beneficial to both male and female dogs. Besides eliminating the possibility of pregnancy, it inhibits (but does not prevent) breast cancer in bitches and prostate cancer in male dogs. Under no circumstances should a

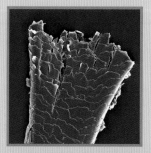
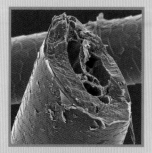

Normal hairs of a dog enlarged 200 times original size. The cuticle (outer covering) is clean and healthy. Unlike human hair that grows from the base, a dog's hair also grows from the end. Damaged hairs and split ends, illustrated above.

SCANNING ELECTRON MICROGRAPHS BY DR. DENNIS KUNKEL, UNIVERSITY OF HAWAII.

DISEASE REFERENCE CHART

	What is it?	What causes it?	Symptoms
Leptospirosis	Severe disease that affects the internal organs; can be spread to people.	A bacterium, which is often carried by rodents, that enters through mucous membranes and spreads quickly throughout the body.	Range from fever, vomiting and loss of appetite in less severe cases to shock, irreversible kidney damage and possibly death in most severe cases.
Rabies	Potentially deadly virus that infects warm-blooded mammals.	Bite from a carrier of the virus, mainly wild animals.	1st stage: dog exhibits change in behavior, fear. 2nd stage: dog's behavior becomes more aggressive. 3rd stage: loss of coordination, trouble with bodily functions.
Parvovirus	Highly contagious virus, potentially deadly.	Ingestion of the virus, which is usually spread through the feces of infected dogs.	Most common: severe diarrhea. Also vomiting, fatigue, lack of appetite.
Canine cough	Contagious respiratory infection.	Combination of types of bacteria and virus. Most common: *Bordetella bronchiseptica* bacteria and parainfluenza virus.	Chronic cough.
Distemper	Disease primarily affecting respiratory and nervous system.	Virus that is related to the human measles virus.	Mild symptoms such as fever, lack of appetite and mucus secretion progress to evidence of brain damage, "hard pad."
Hepatitis	Virus primarily affecting the liver.	Canine adenovirus type I (CAV-1). Enters system when dog breathes in particles.	Lesser symptoms include listlessness, diarrhea, vomiting. More severe symptoms include "blue-eye" (clumps of virus in eye).
Coronavirus	Virus resulting in digestive problems.	Virus is spread through infected dog's feces.	Stomach upset evidenced by lack of appetite, vomiting, diarrhea.

bitch be spayed prior to her first season.

Your vet should provide your puppy with a thorough dental evaluation at six months of age, ascertaining whether all the permanent teeth have erupted properly. A home dental-care regimen should be initiated at six months, including brushing weekly and providing good dental devices (such as nylon bones).

Regular dental care promotes healthy teeth, fresh breath and a longer life.

OVER ONE YEAR OF AGE
Once a year, your full-grown dog should visit the vet for an examination and vaccination boosters, if needed. Some vets recommend blood tests, thyroid level check and dental evaluation to accompany these annual visits. A thor-

ough clinical evaluation by the vet can provide critical background information for your dog. Blood tests are often performed at one year of age, and dental examinations around the third or fourth birthday. In the long run, quality preventative care for your pet can save money, teeth and lives.

SKIN PROBLEMS IN RAT TERRIERS

Veterinarians are consulted by dog owners for skin problems more than any other group of diseases or maladies. Dogs' skin is almost as sensitive as human skin and both suffer almost the same ailments, including acne that can affect Hairless Rat Terriers. For this reason, veterinary dermatology has developed into a specialty practiced by many veterinarians.

Since many skin problems have visual symptoms that are almost identical, it requires the skill of an experienced veterinary dermatologist to identify and cure many of the more severe skin disorders. Pet shops sell many treatments for skin problems but most of the treatments are directed at symptoms and not the underlying problem(s). If your dog is suffering from a skin disorder, you should seek professional assistance as quickly as possible. As with all diseases, the earlier a problem is identified and treated, the more likely is a complete cure.

PARASITE BITES

Many of us are allergic to insect bites. The bites itch, erupt and may even become infected. Dogs have the same reaction to fleas, ticks and/or mites. When an insect lands on you, you have the chance to whisk it away with your hand. Unfortunately, when your dog is bitten by a flea, tick or mite, he can only scratch it away or bite it. By the time the dog has been bitten, the parasite has done some of its damage. It may also have laid eggs to cause further problems in the near future. The itching from parasite bites is probably due to the saliva injected into the site when the parasite sucks the dog's blood.

A SKUNKY PROBLEM

Have you noticed your dog dragging his rump along the floor? If so, it is likely that his anal sacs are impacted or possibly infected. The anal sacs are small pouches located on both sides of the anus under the skin and muscles. They are about the size and shape of a grape and contain a foul-smelling liquid. Their contents are usually emptied when the dog has a bowel movement but, if not emptied completely, they will impact, which will cause your dog much pain. Fortunately, your veterinarian can tend to this problem easily by draining the sacs for the dog. Be aware that your dog might also empty his anal sacs in cases of extreme fright.

PET ADVANTAGES

If you do not intend to show or breed your new puppy, your veterinarian will probably recommend that you spay your female or neuter your male. Some people believe neutering leads to weight gain, but if you feed and exercise your dog properly, this is easily avoided. Spaying or neutering can actually have many positive outcomes, such as:

- training becomes easier, as the dog focuses less on the urge to mate and more on you!
- females are protected from unplanned pregnancy as well as ovarian and uterine cancers.
- males are guarded from testicular tumors and have a reduced risk of developing prostate cancer.

Talk to your vet regarding the right age to spay/neuter and other aspects of the procedure.

AUTO-IMMUNE SKIN CONDITIONS

Auto-immune skin conditions are commonly referred to as being allergic to yourself, while allergies are usually inflammatory reactions to an outside stimulus. Auto-immune diseases cause serious damage to the tissues that are involved.

The best known auto-immune disease is lupus, which affects people as well as dogs. The symptoms are variable and may affect the kidneys, bones, blood chemistry and skin. It can be fatal to both dogs and humans, though it is not thought to be transmissible. It is usually successfully treated with cortisone, prednisone or a similar corticosteroid, but extensive use of these drugs can have harmful side effects.

Just as humans have hay fever, rose fever and other fevers from which they suffer during the pollinating season, many dogs suffer the same allergies. When the pollen count is high, your dog might suffer but don't expect him to sneeze and have a runny nose like a human would. Dogs react to pollen allergies the same way they react to fleas—they scratch and bite themselves. Dogs, like humans, can be tested for allergens. Discuss the testing with your veterinary dermatologist.

FOOD PROBLEMS

FOOD ALLERGIES

Some dogs are allergic to many foods that are best-sellers and highly recommended by breeders and vets. Changing the brand of food that you buy may not eliminate the problem if the element to which the dog is allergic is contained in the new brand.

Recognizing a food allergy is difficult. Humans vomit or have rashes when they eat a food to which they are allergic. Dogs neither vomit nor (usually) develop a rash. They react in the same manner as they do to an airborne or flea allergy; they itch, scratch and bite, thus making the diagnosis extremely difficult. While pollen allergies and parasite bites are usually seasonal, food allergies occur all year.

FOOD INTOLERANCE

Food intolerance is the inability of the dog to completely digest certain foods. For example, puppies that may have done very well on their mother's milk may not do well on cow's milk. The result of this food intolerance may be loose bowels, passing gas and stomach pains. These are the only obvious symptoms of food intolerance and that makes diagnosis difficult.

TREATING FOOD PROBLEMS

It is possible to handle food allergies and food intolerance yourself. Put your dog on a diet that he has never had. Obviously if he has never eaten this new food, he can't have been allergic or intolerant of it. Start with a single ingredient that is not in the dog's diet at the present time. Ingredients like chopped beef or chicken are common in dogs' diets, so try something different like lamb, rabbit or some other source of animal protein. Keep the dog on this diet (with no additives) for a month. If the symptoms of food allergy or intolerance disappear, chances are your dog has a food allergy.

Don't think that the single ingredient cured the problem. You still must find a suitable diet and ascertain which ingredient in the old diet was objectionable. This is most easily done by adding ingredients to the new diet one at a time. Let the dog stay on the modified diet for a month before you add another ingredient. Eventually, you will determine the ingredient that caused the adverse reaction.

An alternative method is to carefully study the ingredients in the diet to which your dog is allergic or intolerant. Identify the main ingredient in this diet and eliminate the main ingredient by buying a different food that does not have that ingredient. Keep experimenting until the symptoms disappear after one month on the new diet.

WHEN TO POSTPONE

While the visit to the vet is costly, it is never advisable to update a vaccination when visiting with a sick or pregnant dog. Vaccinations should be avoided for all elderly dogs. If your dog is showing the signs of any illness or any medical condition, no matter how serious or mild, including skin irritations, do not vaccinate. Likewise, a lame dog should never be vaccinated; any dog undergoing surgery or on any immunosuppressant drugs should not be vaccinated until fully recovered.

First Aid at a Glance

Burns
Place the affected area under cool water; use ice if only a small area is burnt.

Bee stings/Insect bites
Apply ice to relieve swelling; antihistamine dosed properly.

Animal bites
Clean any bleeding area; apply pressure until bleeding subsides; go to the vet.

Spider bites
Use cold compress and a pressurized pack to inhibit venom's spreading.

Antifreeze poisoning
Immediately induce vomiting by using hydrogen peroxide.

Fish hooks
Removal best handled by vet; hook must be cut in order to remove.

Snake bites
Pack ice around bite; contact vet quickly; identify snake for proper antivenin.

Car accident
Move dog from roadway with blanket; seek veterinary aid.

Shock
Calm the dog; keep him warm; seek immediate veterinary help.

Nosebleed
Apply cold compress to the nose; apply pressure to any visible abrasion.

Bleeding
Apply pressure above the area; treat wound by applying a cotton pack.

Heat stroke
Submerge dog in cold bath; cool down with fresh air and water; go to the vet.

Frostbite/Hypothermia
Warm the dog with a warm bath, electric blankets or hot water bottles.

Abrasions
Clean the wound and wash out thoroughly with fresh water; apply antiseptic.

 Remember: an injured dog may attempt to bite a helping hand from fear and confusion. Always muzzle the dog before trying to offer assistance.

A male dog flea, *Ctenocephalides canis.*

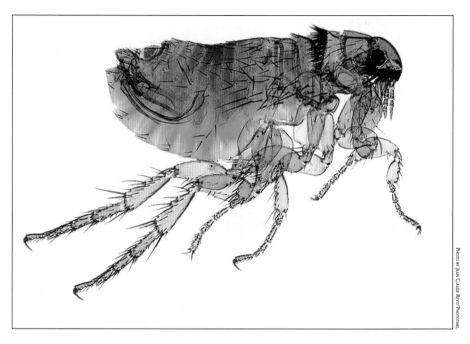

PHOTO BY JEAN CLAUDE REVY/PHOTOTAKE.

EXTERNAL PARASITES

FLEAS

Of all the problems to which dogs are prone, none is more well known and frustrating than fleas. Flea infestation is relatively simple to cure but difficult to prevent. Parasites that are harbored inside the body are a bit more difficult to eradicate but they are easier to control.

To control flea infestation, you have to understand the flea's life cycle. Fleas are often thought of as a summertime problem, but centrally heated homes have changed the patterns and fleas can be found at any time of the year. The most effective method of flea control is a two-stage approach: one stage to kill the adult fleas, and the other to control the development of pre-adult fleas. Unfortunately, no single active ingredient is effective against all stages of the life cycle.

FLEA KILLER CAUTION— "POISON"

Flea-killers are poisonous. You should not spray these toxic chemicals on areas of a dog's body that he licks, including his genitals and his face. Flea killers taken internally are a better answer, but check with your vet in case internal therapy is not advised for your dog.

LIFE CYCLE STAGES

During its life, a flea will pass through four life stages: egg, larva, pupa or nymph and adult. The adult stage is the most visible and irritating stage of the flea life cycle, and this is why the majority of flea-control products concentrate on this stage. The fact is that adult fleas account for only 1% of the total flea population, and the other 99% exist in pre-adult stages, i.e., eggs, larvae and nymphs. The pre-adult stages are barely visible to the naked eye.

THE LIFE CYCLE OF THE FLEA

Eggs are laid on the dog, usually in quantities of about 20 or 30, several times a day. The adult female flea must have a blood meal before each egg-laying session. When first laid, the eggs will cling to the dog's hair, as the eggs are still moist. However, they will quickly dry out and fall from the dog, especially if the dog moves around or scratches. Many eggs will fall off in the dog's favorite area or an area in which he spends a lot of time, such as his bed.

Once the eggs fall from the dog onto the carpet or furniture, they will hatch into larvae. This takes from one to ten days. Larvae are not particularly mobile and will usually travel only a few inches from where they hatch. However, they do have a tendency to move away from bright light and heavy

EN GARDE: CATCHING FLEAS OFF GUARD!

Consider the following ways to arm yourself against fleas:

- Add a small amount of pennyroyal or eucalyptus oil to your dog's bath. These natural remedies repel fleas.
- Supplement your dog's food with fresh garlic (minced or grated) and a hearty amount of brewer's yeast, both of which ward off fleas.
- Use a flea comb on your dog daily. Submerge fleas in a cup of bleach to kill them quickly.
- Confine the dog to only a few rooms to limit the spread of fleas in the home.
- Vacuum daily...and get all of the crevices! Dispose of the bag every few days until the problem is under control.
- Wash your dog's bedding daily. Cover cushions where your dog sleeps with towels, and wash the towels often.

traffic—under furniture and behind doors are common places to find high quantities of flea larvae.

The flea larvae feed on dead organic matter, including adult flea feces, until they are ready to change into adult fleas. Fleas will usually remain as larvae for around seven days. After this period, the larvae will pupate into protective pupae. While inside the pupae, the larvae will undergo metamorphosis and change into adult fleas. This can take as little time as a few days, but the adult fleas can remain inside the pupae waiting to hatch for up to two years. The pupae are signaled to hatch by certain stimuli, such as physical pressure—the pupae's being stepped on, heat from an animal's lying on the pupae or increased carbon-dioxide levels and vibrations—indicating that a suitable host is available.

Once hatched, the adult flea must feed within a few days. Once the adult flea finds a host, it will not leave voluntarily. It only becomes dislodged by grooming or the host animal's scratching. The adult flea will remain on the

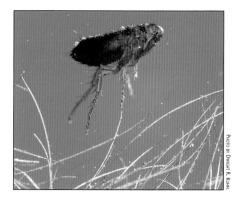

PHOTO BY DWIGHT R. KUHN

host for the duration of its life unless forcibly removed.

TREATING THE ENVIRONMENT AND THE DOG

Treating fleas should be a two-pronged attack. First, the environment needs to be treated; this includes carpets and furniture, especially the dog's bedding and areas underneath furniture. The environment should be treated with a household spray containing an Insect Growth Regulator (IGR) and an insecticide to kill the adult fleas. Most IGRs are effective against eggs and larvae; they actually mimic the fleas' own hormones and stop the eggs and larvae from developing into adult fleas. There are currently no treatments available to attack the pupa stage of the life cycle, so the adult insecticide is used to kill the newly hatched adult fleas before they find a host. Most IGRs are active for many months, while adult insecticides are only active

S. E. M. BY DR DENNIS KUNKEL, UNIVERSITY OF HAWAII.

THE LIFE CYCLE OF THE FLEA

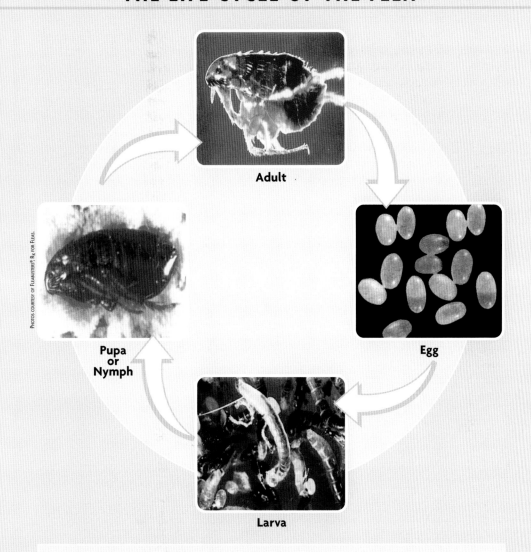

Adult

Egg

Larva

Pupa or Nymph

Fleas have been around for millions of years and have adapted to changing host animals. They are able to go through a complete life cycle in less than one month or they can extend their lives to almost two years by remaining as pupae or cocoons. They do not need blood or any other food for up to 20 months.

INSECT GROWTH REGULATOR (IGR)

Two types of products should be used when treating fleas—a product to treat the pet and a product to treat the home. Adult fleas represent less than 1% of the flea population. The pre-adult fleas (eggs, larvae and pupae) represent more than 99% of the flea population and are found in the environment; it is in the case of pre-adult fleas that products containing an Insect Growth Regulator (IGR) should be used in the home.

IGRs are a new class of compounds used to prevent the development of insects. They do not kill the insect outright, but instead use the insect's biology against it to stop it from completing its growth. Products that contain methoprene are the world's first and leading IGRs. Used to control fleas and other insects, this type of IGR will stop flea larvae from developing and protect the house for up to seven months.

for a few days.

When treating with a household spray, it is a good idea to vacuum before applying the product. This stimulates as many pupae as possible to hatch into adult fleas. The vacuum cleaner should also be treated with an insecticide to prevent the eggs and larvae that have been collected in the vacuum bag from hatching.

The second stage of treatment

is to apply an adult insecticide to the dog. Traditionally, this would be in the form of a collar or a spray, but more recent innovations include digestible insecticides that poison the fleas when they ingest the dog's blood. Alternatively, there are drops that, when placed on the back of the dog's neck, spread throughout the hair and skin to kill adult fleas.

TICKS

Though not as common as fleas, ticks are found all over the tropical and temperate world. They don't bite, like fleas; they harpoon. They dig their sharp proboscis (nose) into the dog's skin and drink the blood. Their only food and drink is dog's

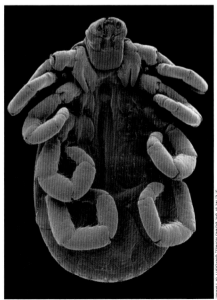

S. E. M. BY DR. DENNIS KUNKEL, UNIVERSITY OF HAWAII

blood. Dogs can get Lyme disease, Rocky Mountain spotted fever, tick bite paralysis and many other diseases from ticks. They may live where fleas are found and they like to hide in cracks or seams in walls. They are controlled the same way fleas are controlled.

The American dog tick, *Dermacentor variabilis*, may well be the most common dog tick in many geographical areas, especially those areas where the climate is hot and humid. Most dog ticks have life expectancies of a week to six months, depending upon climatic conditions. They can neither jump nor fly, but they can crawl slowly and can range up to 16 feet to reach a sleeping or unsuspecting dog.

MITES

Just as fleas and ticks can be problematic for your dog, mites can also lead to an itchy nuisance. Microscopic in size, mites are related to ticks and generally take up permanent residence on their host animal— in this case, your dog! The term *mange* refers to any infestation caused by one of the mighty mites, of which there are six varieties that concern dog owners.

Demodex mites cause a condition known as demodicosis (sometimes called red mange or

DEER-TICK CROSSING

The great outdoors may be fun for your dog, but it also is a home to dangerous ticks. Deer ticks carry a bacterium known as *Borrelia burgdorferi* and are most active in the autumn and spring. When infections are caught early, penicillin and tetracycline are effective antibiotics, but, if left untreated, the bacteria may cause neurological, kidney and cardiac problems as well as long-term trouble with walking and painful joints.

S. E. M. BY DR. ANDREW SPIELMAN/PHOTOTAKE.

PHOTO BY DR. DENNIS KUNKEL, UNIVERSITY OF HAWAII.

The head of an American dog tick, *Dermacentor variabilis*, enlarged and colorized for effect.

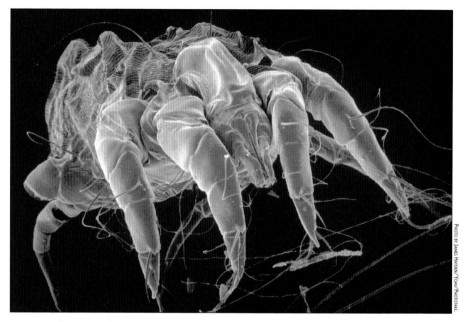

PHOTO BY JAMES HAYDEN/YOAV/PHOTOTAKE.

follicular mange), in which the mites live in the dog's hair follicles and sebaceous glands in larger-than-normal numbers. This type of mange is commonly passed from the dam to her puppies and usually shows up on the puppies' muzzles, though demodicosis is not transferable from one normal dog to another. Most dogs recover from this type of mange without any treatment, though topical therapies are commonly prescribed by the vet.

Human lice look like dog lice; the two are closely related.

PHOTO BY DWIGHT R. KUHN.

The *Cheyletiellosis* mite is the hook-mouthed culprit associated with "walking dandruff," a condition that affects dogs as well as cats and rabbits. This mite lives on the surface of the animal's skin and is readily transferable through direct or indirect contact with an affected animal. The dandruff is present in the form of scaly skin, which may or may not be itchy. If not treated, this mange can affect a whole kennel of dogs and can be spread to humans as well.

The *Sarcoptes* mite causes intense itching on the dog in the form of a condition known as scabies or sarcoptic mange. The cycle of the *Sarcoptes* mite lasts about three weeks, and the mites live in the top layer of the dog's skin (epidermis), preferably in areas with little hair. Scabies is highly contagious and can be passed to humans. Sometimes an allergic reaction to the mite worsens the severe itching associated with sarcoptic mange.

Ear mites, *Otodectes cynotis,* lead to otodectic mange, which most commonly affects the outer ear canal of the dog, though other areas can be affected as well. Dogs with ear-mite infestation commonly scratch at their ears, causing further irritation, and shake their heads. Dark brown droppings in the outer ear confirm the diagnosis. Your vet can prescribe a treatment to flush out the ears and kill any eggs in the ears. A complete month of treatment is necessary to cure the mange.

Two other mites, less common in dogs, include *Dermanyssus gallinae* (the poultry or red mite) and *Eutrombicula alfreddugesi* (the North American mite associated with trombiculidiasis or chigger infestation). The poultry mite frequently lives on chickens, but can transfer to dogs who spend time near farm animals. Chigger infestation affects dogs in the

DO NOT MIX
Never mix parasite-control products without first consulting your vet. Some products can become toxic when combined with others and can cause fatal consequences.

NOT A DROP TO DRINK
Never allow your dog to swim in polluted water or public areas where water quality can be suspect. Even perfectly clear water can harbor parasites, many of which can cause serious to fatal illnesses in canines. Areas inhabited by water-fowl and other wildlife are especially dangerous.

Central US who have exposure to woodlands. The types of mange caused by both of these mites are treatable by vets.

INTERNAL PARASITES
Most animals—fishes, birds and mammals, including dogs and humans—have worms and other parasites that live inside their bodies. According to Dr. Herbert R. Axelrod, the fish pathologist, there are two kinds of parasites: dumb and smart. The smart parasites live in peaceful cooperation with their hosts (symbiosis), while the dumb parasites kill their hosts. Most worm infections are relatively easy to control. If they are not controlled, they weaken the host dog to the point that other medical problems occur, but they do not kill the host as dumb parasites would.

A brown dog tick, *Rhipicephalus sanguineus,* is an uncommon but annoying tick found on dogs.
PHOTO BY CAROLINA BIOLOGICAL SUPPLY/PHOTOTAKE.

Photo by Carolina Biological Supply/Phototake.

The roundworm *Rhabditis* can infect both dogs and humans.

ROUNDWORMS

Average-size dogs can pass 1,360,000 roundworm eggs every day. For example, if there were only 1 million dogs in the world, the world would be saturated with thousands of tons of dog feces. These feces would contain around 15,000,000,000 roundworm eggs.

Up to 31% of home yards and children's sand boxes in the US contain roundworm eggs.

Flushing dog's feces down the toilet is not a safe practice because the usual sewage treatments do not destroy roundworm eggs.

Infected puppies start shedding roundworm eggs at three weeks of age. They can be infected by their mother's milk.

The roundworm, *Ascaris lumbricoides.*

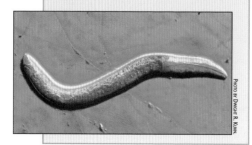

Photo by Dwight R. Kuhn.

ROUNDWORMS

The roundworms that infect dogs are known scientifically as *Toxocara canis.* They live in the dog's intestines and shed eggs continually. It has been estimated that a dog produces about 6 or more ounces of feces every day. Each ounce of feces averages hundreds of thousands of roundworm eggs. There are no known areas in which dogs roam that do not contain roundworm eggs. The greatest danger of roundworms is that they infect people, too! It is wise to have your dog tested regularly for roundworms.

In young puppies, roundworms cause bloated bellies, diarrhea, coughing and vomiting, and are transmitted from the dam (through blood or milk). Affected puppies will not appear as animated as normal puppies. The worms appear spaghetti-like, measuring as long as 6 inches. Adult dogs can acquire roundworms through coprophagia (eating contaminated feces) or by killing rodents that carry roundworms.

Roundworm infection can kill puppies and cause severe problems in adults, as the hatched larvae travel to the lungs and trachea through the bloodstream. Cleanliness is the best preventative for roundworms. Always pick up after your dog and dispose of feces in appropriate receptacles.

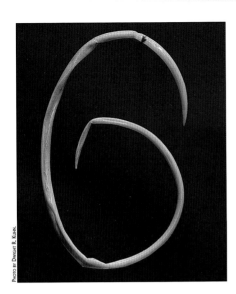

Photo by Dwight R. Kuhn.

The hookworm, *Ancylostoma caninum.*

HOOKWORMS

In the United States, dog owners have to be concerned about four different species of hookworm, the most common and most serious of which is *Ancylostoma caninum,* which prefers warm climates. The others are *Ancylostoma braziliense, Ancylostoma tubaeforme* and *Uncinaria stenocephala,* the latter of which is a concern to dogs living in the Northern US and Canada, as this species prefers cold climates. Hookworms are dangerous to humans as well as to dogs and cats, and can be the cause of severe anemia due to iron deficiency. The worm uses its teeth to attach itself to the dog's intestines and changes the site of its attachment about six times per day. Each time the worm

repositions itself, the dog loses blood and can become anemic. *Ancylostoma caninum* is the most likely of the four species to cause anemia in the dog.

Symptoms of hookworm infection include dark stools, weight loss, general weakness, pale coloration and anemia, as well as possible skin problems. Fortunately, hookworms are easily purged from the affected dog with a number of medications that have proven effective. Discuss these with your vet. Most heartworm preventatives include a hookworm insecticide as well.

Owners also must be aware that hookworms can infect humans, who can acquire the larvae through exposure to contaminated feces. Since the worms cannot complete their life cycle on a human, the worms simply infest the skin and cause irritation. This condition is known as cutaneous larva migrans syndrome. As a preventative, use disposable gloves or a "poop-scoop" to pick up your dog's droppings and prevent your dog (or neighborhood cats) from defecating in children's play areas.

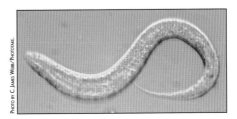

Photo by C. James Webb/Phototake.

The infective stage of the hookworm larva.

TAPEWORMS

Humans, rats, squirrels, foxes, coyotes, wolves and domestic dogs are all susceptible to tapeworm infection. Except in humans, tapeworms are usually not a fatal infection. Infected individuals can harbor 1000 parasitic worms.

Tapeworms, like some other types of worm, are hermaphroditic, meaning male and female in the same worm.

If dogs eat infected rats or mice, or anything else infected with tapeworm, they get the tapeworm disease. One month after attaching to a dog's intestine, the worm starts shedding eggs. These eggs are infective immediately. Infective eggs can live for a few months without a host animal.

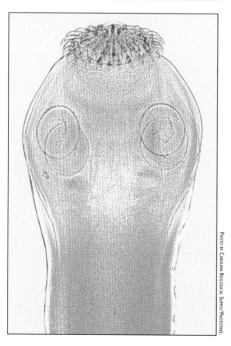

The head and rostellum (the round prominence on the scolex) of a tapeworm, which infects dogs and humans.

PHOTO BY CAROLINA BIOLOGICAL SUPPLY/PHOTOTAKE

TAPEWORMS

There are many species of tapeworm, all of which are carried by fleas! The most common tapeworm affecting dogs is known as *Dipylidium caninum*. The dog eats the flea and starts the tapeworm cycle. Humans can also be infected with tapeworms—so don't eat fleas! Fleas are so small that your dog could pass them onto your hands, your plate or your food and thus make it possible for you to ingest a flea that is carrying tapeworm eggs.

While tapeworm infection is not life-threatening in dogs (smart parasite!), it can be the cause of a very serious liver disease for humans. About 50% of the humans infected with *Echinococcus multilocularis*, a type of tapeworm that causes alveolar hydatid, perish.

WHIPWORMS

In North America, whipworms are counted among the most common parasitic worms in dogs. The whipworm's scientific name is *Trichuris vulpis*. These worms attach themselves in the lower parts of the intestine, where they feed. Affected dogs may only experience upset tummies, colic and diarrhea. These worms, however, can live for months or years in the dog, beginning their larval stage in the small intestine, spending their adult stage in the large intestine and finally passing infective eggs through the dog's feces. The only way to detect whipworms is through a fecal examination, though this is not always foolproof. Treatment for whipworms is tricky, due to the worms' unusual life-cycle pattern, and very often dogs are reinfected due to exposure to infective eggs on the ground. The whipworm eggs can survive in the environment for as long as five years; thus, cleaning up droppings in your own backyard as well as in public places is absolutely essential for sanitation purposes and the health of your dog and others.

THREADWORMS

Though less common than round-worms, hookworms and those previously mentioned, thread-worms concern dog owners in the Southwestern US and Gulf Coast area where the climate is hot and humid. Living in the small intestine of the dog, this worm measures a mere 2 millimeters and is round in shape. Like that of the whipworm, the threadworm's life cycle is very complex and the eggs and larvae are passed through the feces. A deadly disease in humans, *Strongyloides* readily infects people, and the handling of feces is the most common means of transmission. Threadworms are most often seen in young puppies; bloody diarrhea and pneumonia are symptoms. Sick puppies must be isolated and treated immediately; vets recommend a follow-up treatment one month later.

HEARTWORM PREVENTATIVES

There are many heartworm preventatives on the market, many of which are sold at your veterinarian's office. These products can be given daily or monthly, depending on the manufacturer's instructions. All of these preventatives contain chemical insecticides directed at killing heartworms, which leads to some controversy among dog owners. In effect, heartworm preventatives are necessary evils, though you should determine how necessary based on your pet's lifestyle. There is no doubt that heartworm is a dreadful disease that threatens the lives of dogs. However, the likelihood of your dog's being bitten by an infected mosquito is slim in most places, and a mosquito-repellent (or an herbal remedy such as Wormwood or Black Walnut) is much safer for your dog and will not compromise his immune system (the way heartworm preventatives will). Should you decide to use the traditional preventative "medications," you can consider giving the pill every other or third month. Since the toxins in the pill will kill the heartworms at all stages of development, the pill would be effective in killing larvae, nymphs or adults, and it takes four months for the larvae to reach the adult stage. Thus, there is no rationale to poisoning the dog's system on a monthly basis. Lastly, do not give the pill during the winter months, since there are no mosquitoes around to pass on their infection, unless you live in a tropical environment.

Life Cycle of the Heartworm

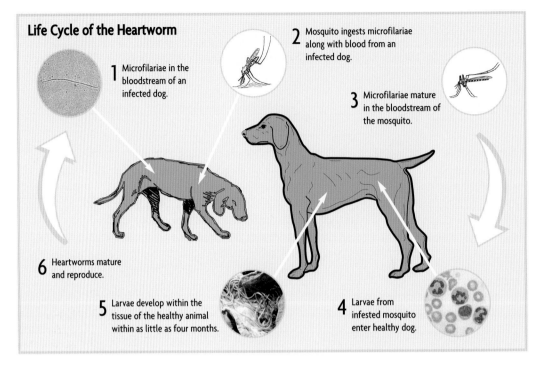

1 Microfilariae in the bloodstream of an infected dog.

2 Mosquito ingests microfilariae along with blood from an infected dog.

3 Microfilariae mature in the bloodstream of the mosquito.

6 Heartworms mature and reproduce.

5 Larvae develop within the tissue of the healthy animal within as little as four months.

4 Larvae from infested mosquito enter healthy dog.

HEARTWORMS

Heartworms are thin, extended worms up to 12 inches long, which live in a dog's heart and the major blood vessels surrounding it. Dogs may have up to 200 worms. Symptoms may be loss of energy, loss of appetite, coughing, the development of a pot belly and anemia.

Heartworms are transmitted by mosquitoes. The mosquito drinks the blood of an infected dog and takes in larvae with the blood. The larvae, called microfilariae, develop within the body of the mosquito and are passed on to the next dog bitten after the larvae mature. It takes two to three weeks for the larvae to develop to the infective stage within the body of the mosquito. Dogs are usually treated at about six weeks of age and maintained on a prophylactic dose given monthly.

Blood testing for heartworms is not necessarily indicative of how seriously your dog is infected. Although this is a dangerous disease, it is not easy for a dog to be infected. Discuss the various preventatives with your vet, as there are many different types now available. Together you can decide on a safe course of prevention for your dog.

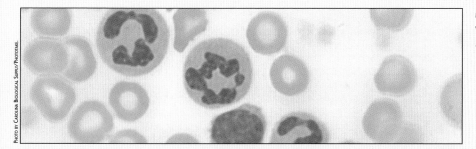

Magnified heart-worm larvae, *Dirofilaria immitis.*

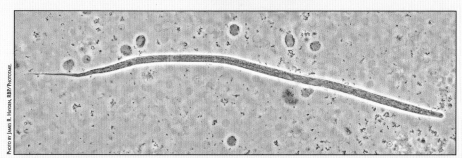

Heartworm, *Dirofilaria immitis.*

The heart of a dog infected with canine heart-worm, *Dirofilaria immitis.*

HOMEOPATHY: an alternative to conventional medicine

"Less is Most"

Using this principle, the strength of a homeopathic remedy is measured by the number of serial dilutions that were undertaken to create it. The greater the number of serial dilutions, the greater the strength of the homeopathic remedy. The potency of a remedy that has been made by making a dilution of 1 part in 100 parts (or 1/100) is 1c or 1cH. If this remedy is subjected to a series of further dilutions, each one being 1/100, a more dilute and stronger remedy is produced. If the remedy is diluted in this way six times, it is called 6c or 6cH. A dilution of 6c is 1 part in 1,000,000,000,000. In general, higher potencies in more frequent doses are better for acute symptoms and lower potencies in more infrequent doses are more useful for chronic, long-standing problems.

CURING OUR DOGS NATURALLY

Holistic medicine means treating the whole animal as a unique, perfect, living being. Generally, holistic treatments do not suppress the symptoms that the body naturally produces, as do most medications prescribed by conventional doctors and vets. Holistic methods seek to cure disease by regaining balance and harmony in the patient's environment. Some of these methods include use of nutritional therapy, herbs, flower essences, aromatherapy, acupuncture, massage, chiropractic and, of course, the most popular holistic approach, homeopathy.

Homeopathy is a theory or system of treating illness with small doses of substances which, if administered in larger quantities, would produce the symptoms that the patient already has. This approach is often described as "like cures like." Although modern veterinary medicine is geared toward the "quick fix," homeopathy relies on the belief that, given the time, the body is able to heal itself and return to its natural, healthy state.

Choosing a remedy to cure a problem in our dogs is the difficult part of homeopathy. Consult with your vet for a professional diagnosis of your dog's symptoms. Often these symptoms require immediate conventional care. If your vet is willing and knowledgeable, you may attempt a homeopathic remedy. Be aware that cortisone prevents homeopathic remedies from working. There are hundreds of possibilities and combinations to cure many problems in dogs, from basic physical problems such as excessive shedding, fleas or other parasites, unattractive doggy odor, bad breath, upset tummy, obesity, dry, oily or dull coat, diarrhea, ear problems or eye discharge (including tears and dry or mucousy matter), to behavioral abnormalities such as fear of loud noises, habitual licking, poor appetite, excessive barking and various phobias. From alumina to zincum metallicum, the remedies span the planet and the imagination…from flowers and weeds to chemicals, insect droppings, diesel smoke and volcanic ash.

Using "Like to Treat Like"

Unlike conventional medicines that suppress symptoms, homeopathic remedies treat illnesses with small doses of substances that, if administered in larger quantities, would produce the symptoms that the patient already has. While the same homeopathic remedy can be used to treat different symptoms in different dogs, here are some interesting remedies and their uses.

Apis Mellifica
(made from honey bee venom) can be used for allergies or to reduce swelling that occurs in acutely infected kidneys.

Diesel Smoke
can be used to help control travel sickness.

Calcarea Fluorica
(made from calcium fluoride, which helps harden bone structure) can be useful in treating hard lumps in tissues.

Natrum Muriaticum
(made from common salt, sodium chloride) is useful in treating thin, thirsty dogs.

Nitricum Acidum
(made from nitric acid) is used for symptoms you would expect to see from contact with acids, such as lesions, especially where the skin joins the linings of body orifices or openings such as the lips and nostrils.

Symphytum
(made from the herb Knitbone, *Symphytum officianale*) is used to encourage bones to heal.

Urtica Urens
(made from the common stinging nettle) is used in treating painful, irritating rashes.

HOMEOPATHIC REMEDIES FOR YOUR DOG

Symptom/Ailment	Possible Remedy
ALLERGIES	Apis Mellifica 30c, Astacus Fluviatilis 6c, Pulsatilla 30c, Urtica Urens 6c
ALOPECIA	Alumina 30c, Lycopodium 30c, Sepia 30c, Thallium 6c
ANAL GLANDS (BLOCKED)	Hepar Sulphuris Calcareum 30c, Sanicula 6c, Silicea 6c
ARTHRITIS	Rhus Toxicodendron 6c, Bryonia Alba 6c
CATARACT	Calcarea Carbonica 6c, Conium Maculatum 6c, Phosphorus 30c, Silicea 30c
CONSTIPATION	Alumina 6c, Carbo Vegetabilis 30c, Graphites 6c, Nitricum Acidum 30c, Silicea 6c
COUGHING	Aconitum Napellus 6c, Belladonna 30c, Hyoscyamus Niger 30c, Phosphorus 30c
DIARRHEA	Arsenicum Album 30c, Aconitum Napellus 6c, Chamomilla 30c, Mercurius Corrosivus 30c
DRY EYE	Zincum Metallicum 30c
EAR PROBLEMS	Aconitum Napellus 30c, Belladonna 30c, Hepar Sulphuris 30c, Tellurium 30c, Psorinum 200c
EYE PROBLEMS	Borax 6c, Aconitum Napellus 30c, Graphites 6c, Staphysagria 6c, Thuja Occidentalis 30c
GLAUCOMA	Aconitum Napellus 30c, Apis Mellifica 6c, Phosphorus 30c
HEAT STROKE	Belladonna 30c, Gelsemium Sempervirens 30c, Sulphur 30c
HICCOUGHS	Cinchona Deficinalis 6c
HIP DYSPLASIA	Colocynthis 6c, Rhus Toxicodendron 6c, Bryonia Alba 6c
INCONTINENCE	Argentum Nitricum 6c, Causticum 30c, Conium Maculatum 30c, Pulsatilla 30c, Sepia 30c
INSECT BITES	Apis Mellifica 30c, Cantharis 30c, Hypericum Perforatum 6c, Urtica Urens 30c
ITCHING	Alumina 30c, Arsenicum Album 30c, Carbo Vegetabilis 30c, Hypericum Perforatum 6c, Mezerium 6c, Sulphur 30c
KENNEL COUGH	Drosera 6c, Ipecacuanha 30c
MASTITIS	Apis Mellifica 30c, Belladonna 30c, Urtica Urens 1m
MOTION SICKNESS	Cocculus 6c, Petroleum 6c
PATELLAR LUXATION	Gelsemium Sempervirens 6c, Rhus Toxicodendron 6c
PENIS PROBLEMS	Aconitum Napellus 30c, Hepar Sulphuris Calcareum 30c, Pulsatilla 30c, Thuja Occidentalis 6c
PUPPY TEETHING	Calcarea Carbonica 6c, Chamomilla 6c, Phytolacca 6c

Recognizing a Sick Dog

Unlike colicky babies and cranky children, our canine kids cannot tell us when they are feeling ill. Therefore, there are a number of signs that owners can identify to know that their dogs are not feeling well.

Take note for physical manifestations such as:

- unusual, bad odor, including bad breath
- excessive shedding
- wax in the ears, chronic ear irritation
- oily, flaky, dull haircoat
- mucus, tearing or similar discharge in the eyes
- fleas or mites
- mucus in stool, diarrhea
- sensitivity to petting or handling
- licking at paws, scratching face, etc.

Keep an eye out for behavioral changes as well including:

- lethargy, idleness
- lack of patience or general irritability
- lack of appetite
- phobias (fear of people, loud noises, etc.)
- strange behavior, suspicion, fear
- coprophagia
- more frequent barking
- whimpering, crying

Get Well Soon

You don't need a DVM to provide good TLC to your sick or recovering dog, but you do need to pay attention to some details that normally wouldn't bother him. The following tips will aid Fido's recovery and get him back on his paws again:

- Keep his space free of irritating smells, like heavy perfumes and air fresheners.
- Rest is the best medicine! Avoid harsh lighting that will prevent your dog from sleeping. Shade him from bright sunlight during the day and dim the lights in the evening.
- Keep the noise level down. Animals are more sensitive to sound when they are sick.
- Be attentive to any necessary temperature adjustments. A dog with a fever needs a cool room and cold liquids. A bitch that is whelping or recovering from surgery will be more comfortable in a warm room, consuming warm liquids and food.
- You wouldn't send a sick child back to school early, so don't rush your dog back into a full routine until he seems absolutely ready.

Number-One Killer Disease in Dogs: CANCER

In every age, there is a word associated with a disease or plague that causes humans to shudder. In the 21st century, that word is "cancer." Just as cancer is the leading cause of death in humans, it claims nearly half the lives of dogs that die from a natural disease as well as half the dogs that die over the age of ten years.

Described as a genetic disease, cancer becomes a greater risk as the dog ages. Vets and dog owners have become increasingly aware of the threat of cancer to dogs. Statistics reveal that one dog in every five will develop cancer, the most common of which is skin cancer. Many cancers, including prostate, ovarian and breast cancer, can be avoided by spaying and neutering our dogs by the age of six months.

Early detection of cancer can save or extend a dog's life, so it is absolutely vital for owners to have their dogs examined by a qualified vet or oncologist immediately upon detection of any abnormality. Certain dietary guidelines have also proven to reduce the onset and spread of cancer. Foods based on fish rather than beef, due to the presence of Omega-3 fatty acids, are recommended. Other amino acids such as glutamine have significant benefits for canines, particularly those breeds that show a greater susceptibility to cancer.

Cancer management and treatments promise hope for future generations of canines. Since the disease is genetic, breeders should never breed a dog whose parents, grandparents and any related siblings have developed cancer. It is difficult to know whether to exclude an otherwise healthy dog from a breeding program, as the disease does not manifest itself until the dog's senior years.

RECOGNIZE CANCER WARNING SIGNS

Since early detection can possibly rescue your dog from becoming a cancer statistic, it is essential for owners to recognize the possible signs and seek the assistance of a qualified professional.

- Abnormal bumps or lumps that continue to grow
- Bleeding or discharge from any body cavity
- Persistent stiffness or lameness
- Recurrent sores or sores that do not heal
- Inappetence
- Breathing difficulties
- Weight loss
- Bad breath or odors
- General malaise and fatigue
- Eating and swallowing problems
- Difficulty urinating and defecating

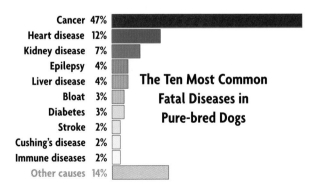

Disease	%
Cancer	47%
Heart disease	12%
Kidney disease	7%
Epilepsy	4%
Liver disease	4%
Bloat	3%
Diabetes	3%
Stroke	2%
Cushing's disease	2%
Immune diseases	2%
Other causes	14%

The Ten Most Common Fatal Diseases in Pure-bred Dogs

CDS: COGNITIVE DYSFUNCTION SYNDROME
"Old-Dog Syndrome"

There are many ways for you to evaluate old-dog syndrome. Veterinarians have defined CDS (cognitive dysfunction syndrome) as the gradual deterioration of cognitive abilities. These are indicated by changes in the dog's behavior. When a dog changes his routine response, and maladies have been eliminated as the cause of these behavioral changes, then CDS is the usual diagnosis.

More than half the dogs over eight years old suffer from some form of CDS. The older the dog, the more chance he has of suffering from CDS. In humans, doctors often dismiss the CDS behavioral changes as part of "winding down."

There are four major signs of CDS: frequent potty accidents inside the home, sleeping much more or much less than normal, acting confused and failing to respond to social stimuli.

SYMPTOMS OF CDS

FREQUENT POTTY ACCIDENTS
- *Urinates in the house.*
- *Defecates in the house.*
- *Doesn't signal that he wants to go out.*

SLEEP PATTERNS
- *Moves much more slowly.*
- *Sleeps more than normal during the day.*
- *Sleeps less during the night.*

CONFUSION
- *Goes outside and just stands there.*
- *Appears confused with a faraway look in his eyes.*
- *Hides more often.*
- *Doesn't recognize friends.*
- *Doesn't come when called.*
- *Walks around listlessly and without a destination.*

FAILURE TO RESPOND TO SOCIAL STIMULI
- *Comes to people less frequently, whether called or not.*
- *Doesn't tolerate petting for more than a short time.*
- *Doesn't come to the door when you return home.*

RAT TERRIER

The term *old* is a qualitative term. For dogs, as well as their masters, old is relative. Certainly we can all distinguish between a puppy Rat Terrier and an adult Rat Terrier— there are the obvious physical traits, such as size, appearance and facial expressions, and personality traits. Puppies and young dogs like to play with children. Children's natural exuberance is a good match for the seemingly endless energy of young dogs. They like to run, jump, chase and retrieve. When dogs grow older and cease their interaction with children, they are often thought of as being too old to play with the kids.

On the other hand, if a Rat Terrier is only exposed to people who lead quieter lifestyles, his life will normally be less active and he will not seem to be getting old as his activity level slows down.

If people live to be 100 years old, dogs live to be 20 years old. While this is a good rule of thumb, it is very inaccurate. When trying to compare dog years to human years, you cannot make a generalization about all dogs. You can make the generalization that 12 to 18 years is a good lifespan for a Rat Terrier, with smaller representatives of the breed living longer than larger ones, though this varies from strain to strain. Dogs are generally considered mature within three years, but they can reproduce even earlier. So the first three years of a dog's life are like seven times that of comparable humans. That means a 3-year-old dog is like a 21-year-old human. As the curve of comparison shows, there is no hard and fast rule for comparing dog and human ages. The comparison is made even more difficult, for not all humans age at the same rate...and human females live longer than human males.

WHAT TO LOOK FOR IN SENIORS

Most vets and behaviorists use the seven-year mark as the time to consider a dog a senior. The term *senior* does not imply that the dog is geriatric and has begun to fail in mind and body. Aging is essentially a slowing process. Humans readily admit that they feel a difference in their activity level from age 20 to 30, and then from 30 to 40, etc. By treating the seven-year-old dog as a senior, owners are able to implement certain therapeutic and preventative medical strategies with the help of their vets. A senior-care program should include at least two veterinary visits per year, screening sessions to determine the dog's health status, as well as nutritional counseling. Veterinarians determine the senior dog's health status through a blood smear for a complete blood count, serum chemistry profile with electrolytes, urinalysis, blood pressure check, electrocardiogram, ocular tonometry (pressure on the eyeball) and dental prophylaxis.

Such an extensive program for senior dogs is well advised before owners start to see the obvious physical signs of aging, such as slower and inhibited movement,

graying, increased sleep/nap periods and disinterest in play and other activity. This preventative program promises a longer, healthier life for the aging dog. Among the physical problems common in aging dogs are the loss of sight and hearing, arthritis, kidney and liver failure, diabetes mellitus, heart disease and Cushing's disease (a hormonal disease).

In addition to the physical manifestations discussed, there are some behavioral changes and problems related to aging dogs. Dogs suffering from hearing or vision loss, dental discomfort or arthritis can become aggressive. Likewise the near-deaf and/or blind dog may be startled more easily and react in an unexpectedly aggressive manner. Seniors suffering from senility can become

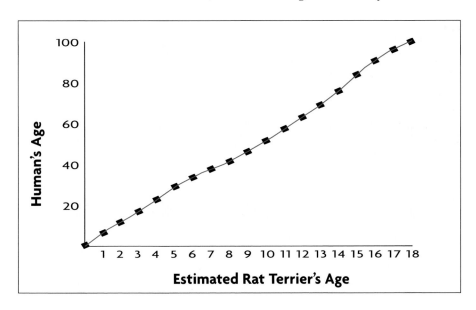

more impatient and irritable. Housesoiling accidents are associated with loss of mobility, kidney problems, loss of sphincter control as well as plaque accumulation, physiological brain changes and reactions to medications. Older dogs, just like young puppies, suffer from separation anxiety, which can lead to excessive barking, whining, housesoiling and destructive behavior. Seniors may become fearful of everyday sounds, such as vacuum cleaners, heaters, thunder and passing traffic. Some dogs have difficulty sleeping, due to discomfort, the need for frequent toilet visits and the like.

Owners should avoid spoiling the older dog with too many fatty treats. Obesity is a common problem in older dogs and subtracts years from their lives. Keep the senior dog as trim as possible since excessive weight puts additional stress on the body's vital organs. Some breeders recommend supplementing the diet with foods high in fiber and lower in calories. Adding fresh vegetables and marrow broth to the senior's diet makes a tasty, low-calorie, low-fat supplement. Vets also offer specialty diets for senior dogs that are worth exploring.

Your dog, as he nears his twilight years, needs his owner's patience and good care more than ever. Never punish an older dog for an accident or abnormal behav-

ior. For all the years of love, protection and companionship that your dog has provided, he deserves special attention and courtesies. The older dog may need to relieve himself at 3 a.m. because he can no longer hold it for eight hours. Older dogs may not be able to remain crated for more than two or three hours. It may be time to give up a sofa or chair to your old friend. Although may not seem as enthusiastic about your attention and petting, he does appreciate the considerations you offer as he gets older.

Your dog does not understand why his world is slowing down. Owners must make the transition into the golden years as pleasant and rewarding as possible.

WHEN THE TIME COMES
You are never fully prepared to make a rational decision about putting your dog to sleep. It is very obvious that you love your Rat Terrier or you would not be reading this book. Putting a loved dog to sleep is extremely difficult. It is a decision that must be made with your veterinarian. You are usually forced to make the decision when one of the life-threatening symptoms above becomes serious enough for you to seek veterinary help.

If the prognosis of the malady indicates the end is near and your beloved pet will only suffer more and experience no enjoyment for the balance of his life, then euthanasia is the right choice.

WHAT IS EUTHANASIA?

Euthanasia derives from the Greek, meaning *good death*. In other words, it means the planned, painless killing of a dog suffering from a painful, incurable condition, or who is so aged that he cannot walk, see, eat or control his excretory functions. Euthanasia is usually accomplished by injection with an overdose of an anesthesia or barbiturate. Aside from the prick of the needle, the experience is usually painless.

MAKING THE DECISION

The decision to euthanize your dog is never easy. The days during which the dog becomes ill and the end occurs can be unusually stressful for you. If this is your first experience with the death of a loved one, you may need the comfort dictated by your religious beliefs. If you are the head of the family and have children, you should have involved them in the decision of putting your Rat Terrier to sleep. Usually your dog can be maintained on drugs for a few days in order to give you ample time to make a decision. During this time, talking with members of your family, friends or even people who have lived through this same experience can ease the burden of your inevitable decision.

THE FINAL RESTING PLACE

Dogs can have some of the same privileges as humans. The remains of your beloved dog can be buried in a pet cemetery, which is generally expensive. Dogs can be buried on your property in a place suitably marked with some stone or newly planted tree or bush. Alternatively, they can be cremated individually and the ashes returned to you. A less expensive option is mass cremation, although, of course, the ashes can not then be returned. Vets can usually arrange the cremation on your behalf. The cost of these options should always be discussed frankly and openly with your vet.

GETTING ANOTHER DOG?

The grief of losing your beloved Rat Terrier will be as lasting as the grief of losing a human friend or relative. In most cases, if your dog died of old age (if there is such a thing), he had slowed down considerably. Keeping in mind the demands of a young "feisty" puppy, are you sure that you want a young puppy to replace him? Perhaps you're better off finding a more mature Rat Terrier, say two to three years of age, which will usually be house-trained and will have an already developed personality. In this case, you can find out if you like each other after just a few hours of being together.

When you purchase your Rat Terrier, you will make it clear to the breeder whether you want one just as a lovable companion and pet, or if you hope to be buying a Rat Terrier with show prospects. No reputable breeder will sell you a young puppy and tell you that it is definitely of show quality, for so much can go wrong during the early months of a puppy's development. If you plan to show, what you will hopefully have acquired is a puppy with "show potential."

To the novice, exhibiting a Rat Terrier in the show ring may look easy, but it takes a lot of hard work and devotion to do top winning at a show such as the prestigious Westminster Kennel Club dog show, not to mention a little luck too!

The first concept that the canine novice learns when watching a dog show is that each dog first competes against members of his own breed. Once the judge has selected the best member of each breed (Best of Breed), provided that the show is judged on a Group system, that chosen dog will compete with other dogs in his group. Finally, the dogs chosen first in each group will compete for Best in Show.

The second concept that you must understand is that the dogs are not actually compared against one another. The judge compares each dog against his breed standard, the written description of the ideal specimen that is approved by the United Kennel Club (UKC). While some early breed standards were indeed based on specific dogs that were famous or popular, many dedicated enthusiasts say that a perfect specimen, as described in the standard, has never walked into a show ring, has never been bred and, to the woe of dog breeders around the globe, does not exist. Breeders attempt to get as close to this ideal as possible with every litter, but theoretically the "perfect" dog is so elusive that it is impossible. (And if the "perfect" dog were born, breeders and judges would never agree that it was indeed "perfect.")

If you are interested in exploring the world of dog showing, your best bet is to join your local breed club or the national club, which is the Rat Terrier Club of

America. These clubs often host both regional and national specialties, shows only for Rat Terriers, which can include conformation as well as obedience, rat racing, going to ground and agility trials. Even if you have no intention of competing with your Rat Terrier, a specialty is like a festival for lovers of the breed who congregate to share their favorite topic: Feists! Clubs also send out newsletters, and some organize training days and seminars in order that people may learn more about their chosen breed. To locate the breed club closest to you, contact the UKC, which furnishes the rules and regulations for many events plus general dog registration and other basic requirements of dog ownership.

There are three kinds of conformation shows: an all-breed show (for all recognized breeds), a specialty show (for one breed only, usually sponsored by the parent club) and a Group show (for all breeds in the Group). At a Group show or all-breed show, the Best of Breed winners from each breed then compete against one another for Group One through Group Four. The judge compares each Best of Breed to his breed standard, and the dog that most closely lives up to the ideal for his breed is selected as Group One. Finally, all the group winners (from the Terrier Group, Hound Group, Toy Group, etc.) compete for Best in Show.

If your Rat Terrier is six months of age or older and registered with the UKC, you can enter him in a dog show where the breed is offered classes. Provided that your Rat Terrier does not have a disqualifying fault, he can compete. Only unaltered dogs can be entered in a dog show, so if you have spayed or neutered your Rat Terrier, your dog cannot compete in conformation shows. The reason for this is simple. Dog shows are the main forum to prove which representatives in a breed are worthy of being bred. Only dogs that have achieved championships should be bred.

CLUB CONTACTS

You can get information about dog shows from the national kennel clubs:

American Kennel Club
5580 Centerview Dr., Raleigh, NC 27606-3390
www.akc.org

United Kennel Club
100 E. Kilgore Road, Kalamazoo, MI 49002
www.ukcdogs.com

Canadian Kennel Club
89 Skyway Ave., Suite 100, Etobicoke, Ontario
M9W 6R4 Canada
www.ckc.ca

The Kennel Club
1-5 Clarges St., Piccadilly,
London W1Y 8AB, UK
www.the-kennel-club.org.uk

Altered dogs, however, can participate in other events such as obedience and agility trials.

Before you actually step into the ring, you would be well advised to sit back and observe the judge's ring procedure. If it is your first time in the ring, do not be over-anxious and run to the front of the line. It is much better to stand back and study how the exhibitor in front of you is performing. The judge asks each handler to "stack" the dog, showing the dog off to his best advantage. The judge will observe the dog from a distance and from different angles, and approach the dog to check his teeth, overall structure, alertness and muscle tone, as well as consider how well the dog "conforms" to the standard. Most importantly, the judge will have the exhibitor move the dog around the ring in some pattern that he should specify (another advantage to not going first, but always listen since some judges change their directions—and the judge is always right!). Finally, the judge will give the dog one last look before moving on to the next exhibitor.

If you are not in the top four in your class at your first show, do not be discouraged. Be patient and consistent, and you may eventually find yourself in a winning line-up. Remember that the winners were once in your shoes and have devoted many

JUST FOR THE FUN OF IT
Rat Terriers can participate in AKC Fun Matches, plus breed clubs often host their own Rat Terrier events, where the dogs compete against each other in conformation, agility, obedience, rat racing and going to ground.

hours and much money to earn the placement. If you find that your dog is losing every time and never getting a nod, it may be time to consider a different dog sport or to just enjoy your Rat Terrier as a pet. Parent clubs offer other events, such as races, agility, tracking, obedience and more, which may be of interest to the owner of a well-trained Rat Terrier.

OBEDIENCE TRIALS
Obedience trials in the US trace back to the early 1930s when organized obedience training was developed to demonstrate how well dog and owner could work together. The pioneer of obedience trials is Mrs. Helen Whitehouse Walker, a Standard Poodle fancier, who designed a series of exercises after the Associated Sheep, Police Army Dog Society of Great Britain. Since the days of Mrs. Walker, obedience trials have grown by leaps and bounds, and today there are over 2,000 trials held in the US every year, with more than 100,000 dogs compet-

ing. Any registered dog can enter an obedience trial, regardless of conformational disqualifications or neutering.

AGILITY TRIALS

Agility is designed so that the handler demonstrates how well the dog can work at his side. The handler directs his dog through an obstacle course that includes jumps as well as tires, the dog walk, weave poles, pipe tunnels, collapsed tunnels, etc. While working their way through the course, the dog must keep one eye and ear on the handler and the rest of his body on the course. The handler gives verbal and hand signals to guide the dog through the course.

The first organization to promote agility trials in the US was the United States Dog Agility Association, Inc. (USDAA), which was established in 1986 and spawned numerous member clubs around the country. The USDAA offers titles to winning dogs.

Three titles are available through the USDAA: Agility Dog (AD), Advanced Agility Dog (AAD) and Master Agility Dog (MAD). The AKC offers Novice Agility (NA), Open Agility (OA), Agility Excellent (AX) and Master Agility Excellent (MX). Beyond these four AKC titles, dogs can win additional ones in "jumper" classes, Jumpers with Weave Novice (NAJ), Open (OAJ) and Excellent (MXJ), which lead to the ultimate title(s): MACH, Master Agility Champion. Dogs can continue to add number designations to the MACH titles, indicating how many times the dog has met the MACH requirements, such as MACH1, MACH2, etc.

Agility is great fun for dog and owner with many rewards for everyone involved. Interested owners should join a training club that has obstacles and experienced agility handlers who can introduce you and your Rat Terrier to the "ropes" (and tires, tunnels, etc.).

Agility trials are terrific fun for Rat Terriers and their owners. This Rat Terrier is maneuvering her way over the A-frame, being coaxed by her proud owner.

RAT TERRIER

As a Rat Terrier owner, you have selected your dog so that you and your loved ones can have a companion, a hunter and exterminator, a friend and a four-legged family member. You invest time, money and effort to care for and train the family's new charge. Of course, this chosen canine behaves perfectly! Well, perfectly like a dog.

THINK LIKE A DOG

Dogs do not think like humans, nor do humans think like dogs, though we try. Unfortunately, a dog is incapable of comprehending how humans think, so the responsibility falls on the owner to adopt a viable canine mindset. Dogs cannot rationalize and only exist in the present moment. Many dog owners make the mistake in training of thinking that they can reprimand their dog for something he did a while ago. Basically, you cannot even reprimand a dog for something he did 20 seconds ago! Either catch him in the act or

Unless you train your dog in basic discipline, like the down/stay, he would not be a very welcome guest at a wedding, especially when he has to pose with the bridal party!

forget it! It is a waste of your and your dog's time—in his mind, you are reprimanding him for whatever he is doing at that moment.

The following behavioral problems represent some which owners most commonly encounter. Every dog is unique and every situation is unique. No author could purport for you to solve your Rat Terrier's problems simply by reading a chapter in a breed book. Here we outline some basic "dogspeak" so that owners' chances of solving behavioral problems are increased. Discuss bad habits with your veterinarian and he can recommend a behavioral specialist to consult in appropriate cases. Since behavioral abnormalities are the main reason owners abandon their pets, we hope that you will make a valiant effort to solve your Rat Terrier's problems. Patience and understanding are virtues that must dwell in every pet-loving household.

AGGRESSION

The Rat Terrier is a non-sparring terrier breed, which means that it is less aggressive towards other dogs than most other terriers. Aggressiveness in dogs, however, tends to be a more individual personality trait than a feature of all dogs in the breed. Given the great variety of genetic

AGGRESSIVE BEHAVIOR
Dog aggression is a serious problem. never give an aggressive dog to someone else. The dog will usually be more aggressive in a new situation where his leadership is unchallenged and unquestioned (in his mind).

material that makes up the Rat Terrier, it is difficult to generalize. Nevertheless, aggression, when not controlled in any dog, always becomes dangerous. An aggressive dog, no matter the size, may lunge at, bite or even attack a person or another dog. Aggressive behavior is not to be tolerated. It is painful for a family to watch their dog become unpredictable in his behavior to the point where they are afraid of him.

While not all aggressive behavior is dangerous, growling, baring teeth, etc., can be frightening. It is important to ascertain why the dog is acting in this manner. Aggression is a display of dominance, and the dog should not have the dominant role in his pack, which is, in this case, your family.

It is important not to challenge an aggressive dog as this could provoke an attack. Observe your Rat Terrier's body language. Does he make direct eye contact and stare? Does he try to make himself as large as possible: ears pricked, chest out, tail erect? Height and size signify authority in a dog pack—being taller or above another dog literally means that he is above in social status. These body signals tell you that your Rat Terrier thinks he is in charge, a problem that needs to be addressed. An aggressive dog is unpredictable; you never know when he is going to strike and what he is going to do. You cannot understand why a dog that is playful one minute is growling the next.

The best solution is to consult a behavioral specialist, one who has experience with the Rat Terrier if possible. Together, perhaps you can pinpoint the cause of your dog's aggression and do something about it. An aggressive dog cannot be trusted,

Nothing is as fun for a Rat Terrier as rolling in the grass!

> **I'M HOME!**
> Dogs left alone for varying lengths of time may often react wildly when their owners return. Sometimes they run, jump, bite, chew, tear things apart, wet themselves, gobble their food or behave in very undisciplined ways. If your dog behaves in this manner upon your return home, allow him to calm down before greeting him or he will consider your attention as a reward for his antics.

and a dog that cannot be trusted is not safe to have as a family pet. If, very unusually, you find that your pet has become untrustworthy and you feel it necessary to seek a new home with a more suitable family and environment, explain fully to the new owners all of your reasons for rehoming the dog to be fair to all concerned. In the very worst case, you will have to consider euthanasia.

DIGGING
Digging, which is seen as a destructive behavior to humans, is actually quite a natural behavior in dogs. The terrier dogs are largely associated with digging, though the Rat Terrier isn't a digging terrier the way the Jack Russell is considered an expert excavator. Nonetheless, any dog's desire to dig can be irrepressible and most frustrating to

his owners. When digging occurs in your garden, it is actually a normal behavior redirected into something the dog can do in his everyday life. In the wild, a dog would be actively seeking food, making his own shelter, etc. He would be using his paws in a purposeful manner for his survival. Since you provide him with food and shelter, he has no need to use his paws for these purposes, and so the energy that he would be using may manifest itself in the form of little holes all over your yard and flower beds.

Perhaps your dog is digging as a reaction to boredom—it is somewhat similar to someone eating a whole bag of chips in front of the TV—because they are there and there is nothing better to do! Basically, the answer is to provide the dog with adequate play and exercise so that his mind and paws are occupied, and so that he feels as if he is doing something useful.

IT'S PLAY TIME

Physical games like pulling contests, wrestling, jumping and teasing should not be encouraged. Inciting a dog's crazy behavior tends to confuse him. The owner has to be able to control his dog at all times. Even in play, your dog has to know that you are the leader and that you decide when to play and when to behave mannerly.

Of course, digging is easiest to control if it is stopped as soon as possible, but it is often hard to catch a dog in the act. If your dog is a compulsive digger and is not easily distracted by other activities, you can designate an area on your property where he is allowed to dig. If you catch him digging in an off-limits area of the yard, immediately bring him to the approved area and praise him for digging there. Keep a close eye on him so that you can catch him in the act— that is the only way to make him understand what is permitted

The dog's nose is thousands of times more sensitive than that of a human. Terriers can detect the scent of a passing rodent and begin scratching and digging to get a more definite whiff.

and what is not. If you take him to a hole he dug an hour ago and tell him "No," he will understand that you are not fond of holes, or dirt, or flowers. If you catch him while he is stifle-deep in your tulips, that is when he will get your message.

SEPARATION ANXIETY

Your Rat Terrier may howl, whine or otherwise vocalize his displeasure at your leaving the house and his being left alone. This is a normal reaction, no different than the child who cries as his mother leaves him on the first day at school. In fact, constant attention can lead to separation anxiety in the first place. If you are constantly making a fuss over your dog, he will come to expect this from you all of the time and it will be more traumatic for him when you are not there. Obviously, you enjoy spending time with your dog, and he thrives on your love and attention. However, it should not become a dependent relationship in which he is heartbroken without you.

One thing you can do to minimize separation anxiety is to make your entrances and exits as low-key as possible. Do not give your dog a long drawn-out goodbye, and do not lavish him with hugs and kisses when you return. This is giving in to the attention that he craves, and it

> **SOUND BITES**
>
> When a dog bites, there is always a good reason for his doing so. Many dogs are trained to protect a person, an area or an object. When that person, area or object is violated, the dog will attack. A dog attacks with his mouth. He has no other means of attack.
>
> Fighting dogs (and there are many breeds which fight) are taught to fight, but they also have a natural instinct to fight. This instinct is normally reserved for other dogs, though unfortunate accidents can occur; for example, when a baby crawls toward a fighting dog and the dog mistakes the crawling child as a potential attacker.
>
> If a dog is a biter for seemingly no reason, if he bites the hand that feeds him or if he snaps at members of your family, see your veterinarian or behaviorist immediately to learn how to modify the dog's behavior.

will only make him miss it more when you are away. Another thing you can try is to give your Rat Terrier a treat when you leave; this will not only keep him occupied and keep his mind off the fact that you have just left but it will also help him associate your leaving with a pleasant experience.

You may have to accustom your dog to being left alone at intervals. Of course, when your dog starts whimpering as you approach the door, your first instinct will be to run to him and comfort him, but do not do it! Eventually he will adjust to your absence. His anxiety stems from being placed in an unfamiliar situation; by familiarizing him with being alone he will learn that he will survive. That is not to say you should purposely leave your dog home alone, but the dog needs to know that while he can depend on you for his care, you do not have to be by his side 24 hours a day.

When the dog is alone in the house, he should be confined to his designated dog-proof area of the house. This should be the area in which he sleeps and already feels comfortable so that he will feel more at ease when he is alone.

BARKING
Admittedly, the Rat Terrier has more to say than many other dogs, given his superior intelligence and superb way of voicing his concerns. Indeed, barking is a dog's way of "talking" and Rat Terriers are indeed contestants to have their own daily talk shows! Rat Terriers have a unique catalog of sounds they use for communication. Listen carefully as it can be somewhat frustrating for the owner of such a talkative fellow to determine what is on his mind. What does the dog mean by his barking?—is

"LONELY WOLF"
The number of dogs that suffer from separation anxiety is on the rise as more and more pet owners find themselves at work all day. New attention is being paid to this problem, which is especially hard to diagnose since it is only evident when the dog is alone. Research is currently being done to help educate dog owners about separation anxiety and how they can help minimize this problem in their dogs.

HE'S PROTECTING YOU

Barking is your dog's way of protecting you. If he barks at a stranger walking past your house, a moving car or a fleeing cat, he is merely exercising his responsibility to protect his pack (*you*) and territory from a perceived intruder. Since the "intruder" usually keeps going, the dog thinks his barking chased it away and he feels fulfilled. This behavior leads your overly vocal friend to believe that he is the "dog in charge."

he excited, happy, frightened or angry? Does he smell a rodent hiding under the floor boards or was there an animal sleeping in his garden within the past eight hours? Whatever it is that the dog is trying to say, he should not be punished for barking. It is only when the barking becomes excessive, and when the excessive barking becomes a bad habit, that the behavior needs to be modified.

Fortunately, Rat Terriers, making excellent alarm dogs, also can use their barks with purpose. If an intruder came into your home in the middle of the night and your Rat Terrier barked a warning, wouldn't you be pleased? You would probably deem your dog a hero, a wonderful guardian and protector of the home. On the other hand, if a friend drops by unexpectedly and rings the doorbell and is greeted with a sudden sharp bark, you would probably be annoyed at the dog. But in reality, isn't this just the same behavior? The dog does not know any better...unless he sees who is at the door and it is someone he knows, he will bark as a means of vocalizing that his (and your) territory is being threatened. While your friend is not posing a threat, it is all the same to the dog. Barking is his means of letting you know that there is an intrusion, whether

Do you think you could train your Rat Terrier to pose for an artist? This photo has, of course, been retouched. But it is so cute that it understandably had to find its way into this book.

friend or foe, on your property. This type of barking is instinctive and should not be discouraged.

DOG TALK

Deciphering your dog's barks is very similar to understanding a baby's cries: there is a different cry for eating, sleeping, potty needs, etc. Your dog talks to you not only through howls and groans but also through his body language. Baring teeth, staring and inflating the chest are all threatening gestures. If a dog greets you by licking his nose, turning his head or yawning, these are friendly, peacemaking gestures.

Excessive habitual barking, however, is a problem that should be corrected early on. As your Rat Terrier grows up, you will be able to tell when his barking is purposeful and when it is for no reason. You will become able to distinguish your dog's different barks and their meanings. For example, the bark when someone comes to the door will be different from the bark when he is excited to see you. It is similar to a person's tone of voice, except that the dog has to rely totally on tone of voice because he does not have the benefit of using words. An incessant barker will be evident at an early age.

PHARMACEUTICAL FIX

There are two drugs specifically designed to treat mental problems in dogs. About seven million dogs each year are destroyed because owners can no longer tolerate their dogs' behavior, according to Nicholas Dodman, a specialist in animal behavior at Tufts University in Massachusetts.

The first drug, Clomicalm, is prescribed for dogs suffering from separation anxiety, which is said to cause them to react when left alone by barking, chewing their owners' belongings, drooling copiously or defecating or urinating inside the home.

The second drug, Anipryl, is recommended for cognitive dysfunction syndrome or "old dog syndrome," a mental deterioration that comes with age. Such dogs often seem to forget that they were housebroken and where their food bowls are, and they may even fail to recognize their owners.

A tremendous human-animal bonding relationship is established with all dogs, particularly senior dogs. This precious relationship deteriorates when the dog does not recognize his master. The drug can restore the bond and make senior dogs feel more like their "old selves."

There are some things that encourage a dog to bark. For example, if your dog barks non-stop for a few minutes and you give him a treat to quiet him, he believes that you are rewarding him for barking. He will associate barking with getting a treat and will keep doing it until he is rewarded.

SEXUAL BEHAVIOR

Dogs exhibit certain sexual behaviors that may have influenced your choice of male or female when you first purchased your Rat Terrier. To a certain extent, spaying/neutering will eliminate these behaviors, but if you are purchasing a dog that you wish to breed from, you should be aware of what you will have to deal with throughout the dog's life.

Female dogs usually have two estruses per year with each season lasting about three weeks. These are the only times in which a female dog will mate, and she usually will not allow this until the second week of the cycle, but this does vary from bitch to bitch. If not bred during the heat cycle, it is not uncommon for a bitch to experience a false pregnancy, in which her mammary glands swell and she exhibits maternal tendencies toward toys or other objects.

Males dogs, likewise, have a number of sexually driven habits with which owners must contend. Marking in and around the house is a common problem of unaltered males. Lifting his leg to squirt a drop of urine is an annoying habit that must be discouraged from the first sign of your little macho Feist's sniffing and raising his little foot! Do not discourage the habit while the dog is outdoors, only when he's about to christen your Chippendale cabinet! Wandering is another habit of males (dogs and humans!), and this must be kept in consideration when allowing the dog outside. Keep your male dog (and your husband) on a tight lead if you ever want to see them again. The search for possible mates propels males to look beyond their own backyard for their next conquest. Mounting is one sign of this seemingly irrepressible need to perpetuate the race, though it is also a sign of dominance. Mounting can be observed in males and females alike, and some females are more aggressive mounters than their male counterparts. Discourage this habit early on: be consistent and persistent and you will find that you can "move mounters," too!

CHEWING

The national canine pastime is chewing! Every dog loves to sink his "canines" into a tasty bone, but sometimes that bone is in his owner's hand! Dogs need to chew, to massage their gums, to

NO KISSES

We all love our dogs and our dogs love us. They show their love and affection by licking us. This is not a very sanitary practice, as dogs lick and sniff in some unsavory places. Kissing your dog on the mouth is strictly forbidden, as parasites can be transmitted in this manner.

Chewing is a normal behavior that all dogs exhibit. Providing enjoyable, durable chew toys will help redirect chewing into positive (non-destructive) directions.

make their new teeth feel better and to exercise their jaws. This is a natural behavior deeply embedded in all things canine. Your role as owner is not to stop the dog's chewing, but to redirect it to positive, chew-worthy objects. Be an informed owner and purchase proper chew toys like strong nylon bones that will not splinter. Be sure that the objects are safe and durable, since your dog's safety is at risk. Again, the owner is responsible for ensuring a dog-proof environment. The best answer is prevention, that is, put your shoes, handbags and other tasty objects in their proper places (out of the reach of the growing canine mouth). Direct puppies to their toys whenever you see them tasting the furniture legs or the leg of your pants. Make a loud noise to attract the pup's attention and immediately escort him to his chew toy and engage him with the toy for at least four minutes, praising and encouraging him all the while.

AIN'T MISBEHAVIN'

Punishment is rarely necessary for a misbehaving dog. Dogs that habitually behave badly probably had a poor education and do not know what is expected of them. They need training. Negative reinforcement on your part usually does more harm than good.

Some trainers recommend deterrents, such as hot pepper, a bitter spice or a product designed for this purpose, to discourage the dog from chewing unwanted objects. Test these products yourself before investing in large quantities.

JUMPING UP

Jumping up is a dog's friendly way of saying hello! Some dog owners do not mind when their dog jumps up. The problem arises when guests come to the house and the dog greets them in the same manner—whether they like it or not! However friendly the greeting may be, the chances are that your visitors will not appreciate your dog's enthusiasm. The dog will not be able to distinguish upon whom he can jump and whom he cannot. Therefore, it is probably best to discourage this behavior entirely.

Pick a command such as "Off" (avoid using "Down" since you will use that for the dog to lie down) and tell him "Off" when he jumps up. Place him on the ground on all fours and have him sit, praising him the whole time. Always lavish him with praise and petting when he is in the sit position. In this way you can give him a warm affectionate greeting, let him know that you are as pleased to see him as he is to see you and instill good manners at the same time!

Owning a Rat Terrier has more rewards than you can imagine...from ribbons and trophies in the show ring to a lifetime of companionship and unconditional love.

Beggars can be fun. But if you reward them for their begging by giving them a treat, you'll have them begging every time they see you.

FOOD STEALING

Is your dog devising ways of stealing food from your coffee table? If so, you must answer the following questions: Is your Rat Terrier hungry or is he "constantly famished" like many dogs seem to be? Face it, some dogs are more food-motivated than others. They are totally obsessed by the smell of food and can only think of their next meal. Food stealing is terrific fun and always yields a great reward—*food*, glorious food.

The owner's goal, therefore, is to be sensible about where food is placed in the home, and to reprimand the dog whenever he is caught in the act of stealing. But remember, only reprimand your dog if you actually see him stealing, not later when the crime is discovered for that will be of no use at all and will only serve to confuse him.

BEGGING

Just like food stealing, begging is a favorite pastime of hungry puppies! It achieves that same terrific result—*food*! Dogs quickly learn that their owners keep the "good food" for ourselves, and that we humans do not dine on dry food alone. Begging is a conditioned response related to a specific stimulus, time and place. The sounds of the kitchen, cans and bottles opening, crinkling bags,

the smell of food in preparation, etc., will excite the dog and soon the paws are in the air!

Here is the solution to stopping this behavior: Never give in to a beggar! You are rewarding the dog for sitting pretty, jumping up, whining and rubbing his nose into you by giving him food. By ignoring the dog, you will (eventually) force the behavior into extinction. Note that the behavior is likely to get

THE ORIGIN OF THE DINNER BELL

The study of animal behavior can be traced back to the 1800s and the renowned psychologist, Pavlov. When it was time for his dogs to eat, Pavlov would ring a bell, then feed the dogs. Pavlov soon discovered that the dogs learned to associate the bell with food and would drool at the sound of a bell. And you thought yours was the only dog obsessed with eating!

NO JUMPING

Stop a dog from jumping up before he jumps. If he is getting ready to jump onto you, simply walk away. If he jumps up on you before you can turn away, lift your knee so that it bumps him in the chest. Do not be forceful. Your dog soon will realize that jumping up is not a productive way of getting attention.

worse before it disappears, so be sure there are not any "softies" in the family who will give in to little "Oliver" every time he whimpers, "More, please."

COPROPHAGIA

Feces eating is, to humans, one of the most disgusting behaviors that our dog could engage in, yet to the dog it is perfectly normal. It is hard for us to understand why a dog would want to eat his own feces. He could be seeking certain nutrients that are missing from his diet; he could be just plain hungry; or he could be attracted by the pleasing (to a dog) scent. While coprophagia most often refers to the dog eating his own feces, a dog may just as likely eat that of another animal as well if he comes across it. Dogs often find the stool of cats and horses more palatable than that of other dogs.

Vets have found that diets with a low digestibility, containing relatively low levels of fiber and high levels of starch, increase coprophagia. Therefore, high-fiber diets may decrease the likelihood of dogs' eating feces. Both the consistency of the stool (how firm it feels in the dog's mouth) and the presence of undigested nutrients increase the likelihood. Once the dog develops diarrhea from feces eating, he will likely stop this distasteful habit.

Correct your Rat Terrier whenever you catch him acting inappropriately. Make the rules clear to him from the beginning.

The determined and industrious Rat Terrier can find mischief in just about anywhere! Keep an eye on your stuff before your Rat Terrier makes off with it.

"X" MARKS THE SPOT

As a pack animal, your dog marks his territory as a way of letting any possible intruders know that this is his space and that he will defend his territory if necessary. Your dog marks by urinating because urine contains pheromones that allow other canines to identify him. While this behavior seems like a nuisance, it speaks volumes about your dog's mental health. Stable, well-trained dogs living in quiet, less populated areas may mark less frequently than less confident dogs inhabiting busy urban areas that attract many possible invaders. If your dog only marks in certain areas in your home, your bed or just the front door, these are the areas he feels obligated to defend. If your dog marks frequently, see your veterinarian or an animal behaviorist.

To discourage this behavior, first make sure that the food you are feeding your dog is nutritionally complete and that he is getting enough food. If changes in his diet do not seem to work, and no medical cause can be found, you will have to modify the behavior through environmental control before it becomes a habit. The best way to prevent your dog from eating his stool is to make it unavailable—clean up after he eliminates and remove any stool from the yard. If it is not there, he cannot eat it.

Reprimanding for stool eating rarely impresses the dog. Vets recommend distracting the dog while he is in the act of stool eating. Coprophagia is seen most frequently in pups 6 to 12 months of age, and usually disappears around the dog's first birthday.

A well-trained, well-loved Rat Terrier is an indescribable joy to his owner and family.

DOGGIE DEMOCRACY

Your dog inherited the pack-leader mentality. He only knows about pecking order. He instinctively wants to be "top dog," but you have to convince him that you are boss. There is no such thing as living in a democracy with your dog. You are the one who makes the rules.

INDEX

My Rat Terrier

PUT YOUR PUPPY'S FIRST PICTURE HERE

Dog's Name _____

Date _____ Photographer _____